THE
Robert Rose
BOOK OF CLASSIC
DESSERTS

THE
Robert Rose
BOOK OF CLASSIC
DESSERTS

Robert
ROSE

THE ROBERT ROSE BOOK OF CLASSIC DESSERTS

Copyright © 1997 Robert Rose Inc.

For complete cataloguing data, see page 6.

DESIGN AND PAGE COMPOSITION:	MATTHEWS COMMUNICATIONS DESIGN
PHOTOGRAPHY:	RICHARD ALLEN
ART DIRECTION, FOOD PHOTOGRAPHY:	DON FERNLEY
PROPS/FOOD STYLIST:	SUSAN RENOUF
MANAGING EDITOR:	PETER MATTHEWS
RECIPE EDITOR:	LESLEIGH LANDRY
INDEXER:	BARBARA SCHON
COLOR SCANS & FILM:	POINTONE GRAPHICS

Cover photo: STRAWBERRY KIWI CREAM CHEESE CHOCOLATE FLAN (PAGE 136)

Distributed in the U.S. by:
Firefly Books (U.S.) Inc.
P.O. Box 1338
Ellicott Station
Buffalo, NY   14205

Distributed in Canada by:
Stoddart Publishing Co. Ltd.
34 Lesmill Road
North York, Ontario
M3B 2T6

ORDER LINES
Tel: (416) 499-8412
Fax: (416) 499-8313

ORDER LINES
Tel: (416) 445-3333
Fax: (416) 445-5967

Published by: Robert Rose Inc. • 156 Duncan Mill Road, Suite 12
Toronto, Ontario, Canada M3B 2N2   Tel: (416) 449-3535

Printed in Canada

234567

Contents

Canadian Cataloguing in Publication Data

The Robert Rose book of classic desserts

Includes index.

ISBN 1-896503-11-X

1. Desserts.   I. Title: Classic desserts.

TX773.R623 1997   641.8'6   C97-931391-0

PHOTO PROP CREDITS

The publisher expresses appreciation to the following suppliers of props used in the food photography appearing in this book:

VILLEROY AND BOSCH LTD., TORONTO	TABLEWARE
BAY FLOWERS, TORONTO	FLOWERS
B.B. BARGOON'S, TORONTO	FABRICS

INTRODUCTION

For the true dessert lover, there's nothing like dining out at a fine restaurant and having the opportunity to choose from an array of spectacular cakes, tarts, mousses and other confections. These are the kinds of desserts that few of us, even the most accomplished amateur chefs, would ever attempt to prepare at home. But now you can, with *The Robert Rose Book of Classic Desserts*.

Like its predecessors, *The Dessert Scene* and *Manhattan's Dessert Scene*, this book brings you an exquisite range of creations from some of North America's top dessert chefs, specially adapted for home cooking. But now we've made these recipes even more accessible, with larger type, metric equivalents for all measurements, and simple step-by-step instructions.

We believe that this book will be an essential reference for anyone who loves desserts. Here you'll find enduring favorites like Crème Caramel, Apricot Soufflé and Baked Alaska — as well as more unusual creations, such as White and Dark Chocolate Mousse Pâté. You'll find, too, that these recipes are remarkably easy to prepare. All have been thoroughly tested in adapting them for the home kitchen, and use ingredients that are easy to find at local supermarkets.

So go ahead, indulge yourself. Enjoy your classic desserts!

— *The Editors of Robert Rose*

DESSERT TIPS

You don't have to be a professional pastry chef to make classic desserts. In fact, if you follow a few basic principles, you'll be successful just about every time.

HOW TO...

Frost a multi-layered cake. The hardest part about frosting cakes with more than 2 layers is that the "in-between" icing tends to slip out. Here's a quick and easy solution: Just place the layers in a springform pan of the same diameter, frosting the top of each layer as you go. Leave the top-most layer unfrosted and place cake in the freezer for a few minutes until set; remove springform pan, then ice the tops and sides.

Get light, fluffy egg whites. First, make sure you separate the eggs cleanly — even a speck of yolk in the whites can ruin your efforts. (Similarly, the bowl and beaters should be absolutely clean.) You'll find eggs easier to separate when they're cold, but egg whites should be allowed to come to room temperature before beating in order to achieve maximum volume.

Make perfect whipped cream. The operative word here is "cold." Be sure that the cream is well chilled. Put the bowl and beaters in the freezer for 30 minutes before you use them. Whip only until stiff peaks are reached (over-beating cream will result in a curdled consistency) and you'll have light, airy whipped cream.

Melt chocolate. Break into smaller pieces and melt in a microwave on Defrost for 2 to 4 minutes, depending on the quantity. You can also use a double boiler over simmering heat. Transfer melted chocolate into a new bowl and let cool slightly before adding eggs, whipping cream, liquors, or whipped egg whites.

Test cakes for doneness. All cake recipes give approximate baking times because ovens, pans and measurements can differ. (For example, nonstick pans can require as much as 25% less baking time.) Therefore, 10 minutes before the given recipe time is up, test cake with a toothpick or tester in the center. If wet, keep checking at 5-minute intervals. Sometimes a little bit of wetness in the middle will yield a moister cake.

Test pies and cheesecakes for doneness. These differ from other cakes because, needing to be moist, a small portion of the center will remain loose.

Unmold a dessert. To get a clean, unbroken surface, dip the bottom of the mold into a larger pan filled with boiling water for 5 seconds. Invert onto serving dish. If unsuccessful, try another 2 to 3 seconds. Note that if the mold is kept in the water too long, the ingredients will melt.

Use a *bain-marie*. Also known as a water bath, this is the best method for cooking custard-type desserts or crustless cheese-cakes. A pan larger than the baking dish is filled halfway with simmering water. This technique ensures the dessert will remain creamy and smooth.

DECORATIVE TOUCHES

Chocolate curls. Use a vegetable peeler, cheese slicer or sharp knife. Hold chocolate chunk in hands for a few minutes to soften. Peel chocolate, turning it around in your hands when one side starts to melt. Store curls in a cool place.

Confectioners' sugar or cocoa. A simple, but effective decoration. Sift over cake.

Fresh or frozen fruit purées. Usually 1 1/2 cups (375 mL) of fresh fruit will yield about 3/4 cup (175 mL) of purée. When using frozen fruit, defrost, making sure that you strain the excess liquid before puréeing.

Fruit, whole. Sliced strawberries or other fruit make excellent decorations. To make *chocolate-glazed strawberries*, melt 3 oz (90 g) chocolate with 1/2 tsp (2 mL) vegetable oil and dip half of strawberry with fork or toothpick into chocolate. Refrigerate until hardened on wax paper.

Glaze, chocolate (ganache). Melt chocolate and measure whipping cream to equal half the amount of chocolate. Add cream and blend. Usually 4 oz (125 g) chocolate will glaze top of 1 cake.

Glaze, jelly. Used to give fruit a sheen. Melt 2 tbsp (25 mL) jelly (preferably apple) and brush over fruit.

Nuts. Toast in oven on cookie sheet at 450° F (230° C) or in dry skillet over high heat on stove, until golden brown. Grind into desired texture.

If at all possible, try to use the ingredients called for in each recipe. But in a crisis, you can use the following substitutes.

Butter. If butter is not the main ingredient, then margarine, vegetable shortening or lard is an acceptable alternative. In desserts where butter *is* the main ingredient — pound cakes, for example — substitutions may alter the taste greatly.

Cheese. If cheesecakes call for cream cheese, substitute solid cottage cheese that has been well drained. The result will be lighter, but less creamy.

Chocolate. Use cocoa instead, but flavor will not be as rich. To replace 1 oz (25 g) semi-sweet chocolate, use 1 tbsp (15 mL) sugar, 2 1/2 tsp (12 mL) butter and 1 1/2 tbsp (22 mL) cocoa.

Cream. Whipping (35%) cream and *crème fraîche* can be substituted for one another. If light cream is needed, you can use heavy cream, diluting it with half the amount of water. Do not substitute lighter creams for whipping cream.

Sour cream. For a lighter version, substitute unflavored yogurt or buttermilk. However, sour cream has a higher fat content and will produce a richer-tasting dessert.

Electric mixer. Use for whipping, creaming, beating or stirring. Gives greater volume to eggs, butter and sugar.

Food processor. Great for grinding, beating and mixing. Be sure to avoid overprocessing. Do not use for whipping egg whites or cream unless you have a special attachment.

Various pans, including:
Bundt or tube pans — useful for pound, fruit and coffee cakes; the 8-cup (2 L) size is the most common size.
Decorative mold pans — essential for mousses.
Springform pans — a deep cake pan with a removable side. Keep a range of sizes on hand.
Large cake pans — 8- to 9-inch (1.2 or 1.5 L) round pans are useful, especially when lined with parchment paper. A springform pan can replace a cake pan when greater depth is needed.
Jelly roll pans — useful for sponge recipes. Line with buttered, floured parchment paper.

Chocolate

WHITE AND DARK CHOCOLATE MARBLED MOUSSE CAKE

SERVES 12

TIP

It's easier to separate eggs when they're cold.

Egg whites beat to a greater volume when at room temperature.

12-inch (4 L) springform pan

CRUST:

1 cup	chocolate wafer crumbs	250 mL
3 tbsp	melted butter	45 mL

CHOCOLATE FILLING:

14 oz	semi-sweet chocolate, chopped	425 g
2	eggs	2
4	eggs, separated	4
2 cups	whipping (35%) cream	500 mL

WHITE CHOCOLATE MOUSSE:

2 1/2 oz	white chocolate	75 g
2	eggs, separated	2
1/2 cup	whipping (35%) cream	125 mL

1. Make the crust: In a bowl, combine chocolate wafer crumbs and melted butter. Pat onto bottom of pan. Chill while preparing filling.

2. Make the chocolate filling: In a bowl, melt the chocolate over hot (not boiling) water, stirring until smooth; remove from heat. Beat in eggs and egg yolks. In another bowl, beat egg whites until stiff peaks form. In a separate bowl, whip cream until soft peaks form. Alternately fold whites and whipped cream into chocolate mixture. Pour into crust; set aside.

3. Make the white chocolate mousse: In a bowl, melt the white chocolate over hot (not boiling) water, stirring until smooth; remove from heat. Beat in egg yolks. In another bowl, beat egg whites until stiff peaks form. In a separate bowl, whip cream until soft peaks form. Alternately fold whites and whipped cream into white chocolate mixture. Pour into centre of dark chocolate mousse. With a knife swirl white mousse through dark mousse. Chill 3 to 4 hours before serving.

The Quilted Giraffe
– New York

CHOCOLATE CINNAMON CRESCENTS (CHOCOLATE RUGELACH)

MAKES 36

TIP

You can use light cream cheese instead of regular for a lower-calorie treat.

Preheat oven to 375° F (190° C)

Two baking sheets, buttered and floured

3/4 cup	butter	175 mL
6 oz	cream cheese	175 g
1/4 cup	icing sugar	50 mL
1/2 tsp	vanilla extract	2 mL
2 cups	all-purpose flour (approximate)	500 mL
2 tbsp	melted butter	25 mL
2/3 cup	ground nuts	150 mL
1/3 cup	raisins	75 mL
2 tbsp	cinnamon	25 mL
1/3 cup	granulated sugar	75 mL
1/2 cup	chocolate chips	125 mL

1. In a bowl, cream butter with cream cheese; beat in icing sugar and vanilla. Beat in enough flour to make a dough that is not sticky. Divide dough into 3 parts.

2. On a floured board, roll each section of dough into a circle 1/8 inch (2 mm) thick. Brush with melted butter. Sprinkle circles evenly with nuts, then with raisins, cinnamon, sugar and chocolate chips. Cut each circle, pie-fashion, into 12 wedges. Roll each wedge up tightly from wide edge to point and transfer to baking sheet.

3. Bake 20 minutes or until golden.

The Carnegie Delicatessen – Manhattan

CHOCOLATE MOUSSE LAYER CAKE

SERVES 14 TO 16

TIP

Decorate with chocolate shavings or icing sugar.

It's easier to separate eggs when they're cold. Egg whites beat to a greater volume when at room temperature.

Substitute your favorite liqueur for the Grand Marnier.

Preheat oven to 350° F (180° C)

Two 8- or 9-inch (1.2 or 1.5 L) round cake pans, bottoms lined with parchment paper, buttered and floured

CAKE:

1 cup	boiling water	250 mL
1/2 cup	cocoa	125 mL
1 cup	granulated sugar	250 mL
1/2 cup	butter	125 mL
2	eggs	2
1 cup + 2 tbsp	all-purpose flour	275 mL
3/4 tsp	baking soda	4 mL
1/4 tsp	baking powder	1 mL

MOUSSE:

8 oz	semi-sweet chocolate, chopped	250 g
1/4 cup	Grand Marnier	50 mL
4	eggs, separated	4
1 cup	whipping (35%) cream	250 mL

GANACHE:

12 oz	semi-sweet chocolate, chopped (or 2 cups [500 mL] chocolate chips)	375 g
1 cup	whipping (35%) cream	250 mL

1. Make the cake: In a large bowl, stir together boiling water and cocoa until dissolved. In a separate bowl, cream sugar with butter until fluffy; add eggs, one at a time, beating well after each. Add to cocoa mixture, whisking until well-mixed. Stir together flour, baking soda and baking powder; fold into cocoa mixture. Divide batter between prepared cake pans. Bake 20 to 25 minutes or until tester inserted in center comes out clean. Cool in pans on wire racks.

The Silver Palate
– Manhattan

2. Make the mousse: In a bowl, melt the chocolate over hot (not boiling) water, stirring until smooth; remove from heat. Beat in Grand Marnier and egg yolks. In another bowl, beat egg whites until stiff peaks form. In a separate bowl, whip cream until stiff peaks form. Alternately fold whites and whipped cream into chocolate mixture. Chill 30 minutes or until it is of spreading consistency.

3. Make the ganache: In a bowl, melt the chocolate over hot (not boiling) water, stirring until smooth. Beat cream into chocolate until smooth and combined. If ganache hardens before use, reheat slightly until it is of spreading consistency; if ganache is not stiff enough to glaze, chill for a short time.

4. Assembly: Invert cakes; cut each horizontally into 2 layers. Put one layer on serving platter; spread with mousse. Top with another cake layer; spread with mousse. Repeat twice. Ice sides and top with a thin layer of mousse; chill until mousse feels firm. Glaze with ganache.

GRAND MARNIER CHOCOLATE TRUFFLE TORTE

SERVES 10 TO 12

Preheat oven to 350° F (180° C)

**9-inch (2.5 L) springform pan and
9-inch (1.5 L) round cake pan,
bottoms lined with parchment paper, buttered and floured**

TIP

It's easier to separate eggs when they're cold. Egg whites beat to a greater volume when at room temperature.

Substitute your favorite liqueur for the Grand Marnier.

SUGAR DOUGH CRUST:

1/3 cup	butter	75 mL
1/3 cup	granulated sugar	75 mL
2 tbsp	beaten egg	25 mL
1 1/3 cups	all-purpose flour	325 mL
1 1/2 tbsp	cocoa	22 mL
1 tbsp	water	15 mL

TORTE:

3 1/2 oz	semi-sweet chocolate, chopped	110 g
1/4 cup	butter	50 mL
2 1/2 tbsp	granulated sugar	32 mL
3	eggs	3
2	eggs, separated	2
2 tbsp	all-purpose flour	25 mL
1 tbsp	granulated sugar	15 mL

CHOCOLATE TRUFFLE FILLING:

2 cups	whipping (35%) cream	500 mL
7 oz	semi-sweet chocolate, chopped	210 g
1 tbsp	Grand Marnier	15 mL
1 tsp	gelatin	5 mL
	Icing sugar	

1. Make the sugar dough crust: In a bowl, cream butter with sugar until fluffy; beat in egg. In a separate bowl, sift together flour and cocoa; fold into creamed mixture. Stir in water until dough forms. Pat into bottom of springform pan; chill while preparing torte.

2. Make the torte: In a bowl, melt chocolate over hot (not boiling) water, stirring until smooth; cool. In another bowl cream butter with 2 1/2 tbsp (32 mL) sugar until fluffy; beat in cooled chocolate, whole

*The Carnegie
Delicatessen–Manhattan*

eggs and egg yolks. Fold in flour. In a separate bowl, beat egg whites until soft peaks form; gradually add 1 tbsp (15 mL) sugar, beating until stiff peaks form. Fold beaten egg whites into chocolate mixture. Pour batter into cake pan. Bake 30 to 40 minutes or until tester inserted in center comes out clean. Cool on wire rack.

3. Bake sugar dough crust 20 to 25 minutes or until tester inserted in center comes out clean. Cool on wire rack.

4. Make the chocolate truffle filling: In a bowl, whip cream until stiff peaks form. In a separate bowl, melt chocolate over hot (not boiling) water, stirring until smooth; remove from heat and stir in Grand Marnier. Dissolve gelatin in water according to package directions; stir into chocolate. Fold whipped cream into cooled chocolate mixture.

5. Assembly: Cut torte horizontally into 2 layers. Pour one-third of the truffle filling over sugar dough crust in springform pan. Carefully top with one torte layer, then half of remaining truffle filling. Repeat layers. Chill 2 to 3 hours before serving.

6. To serve, unmold. Dust with sifted icing sugar.

KAHLUA TRUFFLE CAKE

SERVES 8 TO 10

TIP

When melting chocolate in a bowl over hot water, don't let the water boil and don't let the bowl touch the water — if the water boils or comes into contact with the bowl, the chocolate can scorch.

Preheat oven to 350° F (180° C)

9-inch (2.5 L) springform pan, bottom lined with buttered parchment paper

CHOCOLATE SPONGE:

3	eggs, separated	3
1/2 cup	granulated sugar	125 mL
1 tsp	vanilla extract	5 mL
1 1/2 tbsp	cocoa	22 mL
1 tbsp	all-purpose flour	15 mL

DESSERT SYRUP:

1/4 cup	water	50 mL
1/4 cup	granulated sugar	50 mL

TRUFFLE FILLING:

8 oz	semi-sweet chocolate, chopped	250 g
3/4 cup	butter	175 mL
1/2 cup	icing sugar	125 mL
1/4 cup	cocoa	50 mL
1/4 cup	Kahlua	50 mL
1	egg	1
1 cup	whipping (35%) cream, at room temperature	250 mL

GANACHE:

6 oz	semi-sweet chocolate, chopped	175 g
1/2 cup	whipping (35%) cream	125 mL
	Sliced toasted almonds	

1. Make the chocolate sponge: Beat egg yolks with 1/4 cup (50 mL) of the sugar until thick and pale yellow, about 2 minutes; beat in vanilla. Gently fold in cocoa and flour. In a separate bowl, beat egg whites until soft peaks form; gradually add remaining 1/4 cup (50 mL) sugar, beating until stiff peaks form. Fold egg whites into batter. Pour into pan. Bake 20 minutes or until tester inserted in center comes out clean. Cool in pan on wire rack.

Baker Street – Toronto

2. Make the dessert syrup: In a small saucepan, combine water and sugar. Bring to a boil; cook until sugar dissolves (do not stir). Set aside to cool.

3. Make the truffle filling: In a bowl, melt the chocolate over hot (not boiling) water, stirring until smooth; set aside. In a separate bowl, beat butter with icing sugar until soft and creamy; beat in cocoa and Kahlua. Add cooled chocolate, beating until well-mixed. Beat in egg. Gradually beat in cream until smooth; set aside.

4. Make the ganache: In a bowl, melt the chocolate over hot (not boiling) water, stirring until smooth. Beat cream into chocolate until smooth and combined. If ganache hardens before use, reheat slightly until it is of spreading consistency; if ganache is not stiff enough to glaze, chill for a short time.

5. Assembly: Brush sponge cake with dessert syrup. Pour truffle filling on top and level. Chill for 1 hour or until firm. Pour ganache over top. Sprinkle with almonds.

SWISS CHOCOLATE LAYERED MOUSSE CAKE

TIP

It's easiest to separate eggs when they are cold, straight from the refrigerator.

Use clean beaters and bowl when beating egg whites.

Preheat oven to 400° F (200° C)

Two 9-inch (1.5 L) round cake pans, lined with parchment paper, buttered and floured

9-inch (2.5 L) springform pan

CAKE:

1 cup	butter, softened	250 mL
1 1/2 cups	granulated sugar	375 mL
2	egg whites	2
2 cups	sifted cake and pastry flour	500 mL
2 1/2 tsp	baking powder	12 mL
1/4 tsp	salt	1 mL
1 cup	milk	250 mL
1 tsp	vanilla extract	5 mL
3	egg whites	3
1 tsp	granulated sugar	5 mL

SYRUP:

1/2 cup	water	125 mL
1/4 cup	granulated sugar	50 mL
	Liqueur, any flavor, to taste	

MOUSSE:

1 lb	semi-sweet Swiss chocolate, chopped	500 g
1 1/3 cups	butter	325 mL
8	eggs, separated	8
2 tsp	gelatin	10 mL
1 cup	whipping (35%) cream	250 mL
1/2 cup	granulated sugar	125 mL
	Chocolate curls	

1. Make the cake: In a large bowl, cream butter with 1 1/2 cups (375 mL) sugar until fluffy; beat in 2 egg whites until light. In another bowl, sift together cake and pastry flour, baking powder and salt. In a separate small bowl, combine milk and vanilla. Alternately add

Dufflet – Toronto

flour mixture and milk mixture to butter mixture, beginning and ending with flour and stirring just until combined. In a separate bowl, beat egg whites until soft peaks form; gradually add sugar, beating until stiff peaks form. Stir one-quarter of egg whites into batter; gently fold in remaining egg whites. Divide batter between prepared cake pans. Bake 25 to 30 minutes or until cake pulls away from side of pan and a cake tester inserted in the center comes out clean. Cool in pans on wire rack.

2. Make the syrup: In a small saucepan bring water and sugar to a boil. Cool. Stir in liqueur to taste.

3. Make the mousse: In a bowl, melt chocolate with butter over hot (not boiling) water, stirring until smooth; cool. Beat egg yolks; blend into chocolate. Dissolve gelatin according to package directions; stir into chocolate mixture. In a bowl, whip cream until stiff peaks form. In a separate bowl, beat egg whites until soft peaks form; gradually add sugar, beating until stiff peaks form. Stir one-quarter of egg whites into chocolate mixture; gently fold in remaining egg whites and whipped cream. Chill.

4. Assembly: Unmold cakes; cut each cake horizontally into 2 layers. Place one layer into springform pan; brush with syrup. Spread with mousse. Repeat twice. Top with remaining cake layer. Refrigerate cake and remaining mousse until mousse sets. Unmold cake; ice top and sides with remaining mousse. Decorate with chocolate curls.

SWISS CHOCOLATE FONDUE

SERVES 4

TIP

This recipe is easily doubled if you're serving a crowd.

3 oz	semi-sweet chocolate, chopped	90 g
3 oz	milk chocolate, chopped	90 g
1/2 cup	whipping (35%) cream, warmed	125 mL
1 tsp	cognac *or* kirsch *or* rum	5 mL

DIPPING FRUITS:

Mandarin orange sections

Pineapple chunks

Strawberries

Sliced apples

Banana chunks

1. In a bowl over hot (not boiling) water, melt milk chocolate and semi-sweet chocolate, stirring until smooth. Stir in cream and cognac. Leave over hot water or transfer to fondue set to serve warm. Serve with assortment of fruit.

Chalet Suisse –
Manhattan

WHITE CHOCOLATE GRAND MARNIER TRUFFLES

MAKES ABOUT 24

TIP

Hold each truffle between two forks and dip into melted white chocolate, letting excess chocolate drip back into bowl.

To decorate truffles, melt a little bitter-sweet or milk chocolate over hot water, stirring until smooth; dip a fork into the melted chocolate and drizzle over chilled truffles.

1/3 cup	whipping (35%) cream	75 mL
1 lb	white chocolate, chopped	500 g
2 tbsp	butter, softened	25 mL
2 tbsp	Grand Marnier	25 mL

1. In a saucepan, heat cream until almost boiling. Cool to room temperature.

2. In a bowl, melt half the white chocolate over hot (not boiling) water, stirring until smooth; remove from heat. Beat in butter. Beat in cream vigorously until mixture is light and fluffy. Beat in Grand Marnier. Chill 1 to 2 hours or until firm.

3. Roll truffle mixture into balls. In a bowl, melt remaining chocolate over hot (not boiling) water, stirring until smooth. Dip truffles in melted chocolate. Place on waxed paper and chill until firm. Store in refrigerator.

Bear Essentials –
Toronto

COINTREAU CHOCOLATE DECADENCE

SERVES 14 TO 16

10- to 12-inch (3 to 4 L) springform pan

CRUST:

1 cup	chocolate wafer crumbs	250 mL
3 tbsp	melted butter	45 mL

FILLING:

1 lb	semi-sweet chocolate, chopped	500 g
10	egg yolks	10
1/3 cup	granulated sugar	75 mL
1	pkg (1 tbsp [7 g]) gelatin	1
1/3 cup	Cointreau or other orange flavored liqueur	75 mL
2 1/2 cups	whipping (35%) cream	625 mL

GANACHE:

12 oz	semi-sweet chocolate, chopped	375 g
3/4 cup	whipping (35%) cream	175 mL
	Large chocolate curls (optional)	

1. Make the crust: In a bowl, combine chocolate wafer crumbs and melted butter. Pat onto bottom of pan. Chill while making filling.

2. Make the filling: In a bowl, melt chocolate over hot (not boiling) water, stirring until smooth; cool slightly. In another bowl, beat egg yolks and sugar until pale yellow and thick; beat in chocolate until blended. Dissolve gelatin in water according to package directions; stir into chocolate mixture. In a separate bowl, whip cream until stiff peaks form; fold gently into chocolate mixture. Pour into crust. Freeze until the top is set.

3. Make the ganache: In a bowl, melt chocolate over hot (not boiling) water, stirring until smooth; cool slightly. Slowly beat in cream. If ganache hardens before use, reheat slightly until it is of spreading consistency; if ganache is not stiff enough to glaze, chill for a short time.

Inn on the Park — Toronto

4. Assembly: Unmold dessert; transfer to a serving platter. Glaze top and sides with ganache. Decorate with large chocolate curls, if desired.

COINTREAU CHOCOLATE CREAM WITH MERINGUE

SERVES 6 TO 8

TIP

Eggs separate more easily when cold — use three bowls, one to separate eggs over, one for the yolks and one to transfer perfectly clean whites to. Make sure there's not a speck of yolk in the whites or they won't beat properly.

Use perfectly clean bowls and beaters when making meringue — just a trace of oil can prevent the egg whites from beating properly.

Preheat oven to 350° F (180° C)

9-inch (2.5 L) springform pan

3 baking sheets lined with parchment paper

MERINGUE:

6	egg whites	6
1 cup	granulated sugar	250 mL
1 cup	ground hazelnuts	250 mL
1/4 cup	all-purpose flour	50 mL

FILLING:

2 1/2 oz	semi-sweet chocolate, chopped	75 g
2 tbsp	Cointreau or other orange flavored liqueur	25 mL
1/2 cup	chocolate chips	125 mL
1/2 cup	chopped toasted almonds	125 mL
1/2 cup	chopped toasted hazelnuts	125 mL
3 cups	whipping (35%) cream	750 mL
3/4 cup	granulated sugar	175 mL
	Sifted icing sugar	
	Chocolate curls	

1. Make the meringue: Using the base of springform pan as a template, draw a 9-inch (23 cm) circle on each piece of parchment paper. Butter parchment circles. In a large bowl, beat egg whites until soft peaks form; gradually add sugar, beating until stiff peaks form. Gently fold in hazelnuts and flour. Spoon meringue onto parchment circles (alternately, pipe mixture spiral-fashion onto circles). Bake for 10 minutes. Cool on wire racks.

Windsor Arms Hotel – Toronto

2. Make the filling: In a bowl, melt chocolate over hot (not boiling) water, stirring until smooth; beat in Cointreau. Cool. In another bowl, stir together chocolate chips, almonds and hazelnuts; set aside. In a separate bowl, whip cream until it starts to thicken; gradually add sugar, beating until stiff peaks form. Stir half of the whipped cream into cooled chocolate-Cointreau mixture; stir remaining whipped cream into chocolate chip-nut mixture.

3. Assembly: Place one meringue in springform pan; spread with chocolate chip-nut whipped cream. Top with another meringue; spread with chocolate-Cointreau whipped cream. Top with final meringue. Refrigerate until cold. Before serving, decorate with sifted icing sugar and chocolate curls.

TRUFFLE CAKE

SERVES 8 TO 10

TIP

Cream whips to a greater volume if the cream, bowl and beaters are all chilled.

Preheat oven to 350° F (180° C)

9-inch (2.5 L) springform pan, buttered

SPONGE:

4	eggs	4
3/4 cup	granulated sugar	175 mL
1/3 cup	all-purpose flour	75 mL
1/4 cup	cocoa	50 mL
2 tsp	cornstarch	10 mL

SYRUP:

1/2 cup	water	125 mL
1/4 cup	granulated sugar	50 mL

FILLING:

7 oz	semi-sweet chocolate, chopped	210 g
1 1/2 cups	whipping (35%) cream	375 mL
	Toasted sliced almonds (optional)	

1. Make the sponge: In a bowl, beat eggs with sugar until thick and pale yellow, about 5 minutes. In a separate bowl sift together flour, cocoa and corn-starch; fold into egg mixture. Pour into prepared pan. Bake 25 to 30 minutes or until cake tester inserted in center comes out clean. Cool in pan on wire rack.

2. Make the syrup: In a small saucepan, bring water and sugar to a boil; boil 2 minutes. Cool.

3. Make the filling: In a bowl, melt the chocolate over hot (not boiling) water, stirring until smooth; cool. In a bowl whip cream until stiff peaks form; fold into cooled chocolate.

L'Hotel – Toronto

4. Assembly: Remove ring of springform pan. Cut cake horizontally into 2 layers; remove upper layer and replace springform ring. Brush bottom layer with syrup. Pour in chocolate filling. Chill 1 hour or until firm. Finely crumble remaining sponge layer and sprinkle on top of cake. Unmold. Decorate sides with toasted sliced almonds, if desired.

NUT TRUFFLES

MAKES ABOUT 24

TIP

Toast nuts in a nonstick skillet over medium-high heat, stirring occasionally, until golden and fragrant. Or, toast in a 350° F (180° C) oven for about 10 minutes.

Substitute your favorite nut for the almonds.

4 oz	milk chocolate, chopped	125 g
4 oz	semi-sweet chocolate, chopped	125 g
1/2 cup	butter, softened	125 mL
1/4 cup	finely chopped toasted almonds	50 mL
1/2 cup	coarsely chopped toasted almonds	125 mL

1. In a bowl, melt milk chocolate and semi-sweet chocolate over hot (not boiling) water, stirring until smooth. Beat in butter vigorously until light and fluffy. Stir in finely chopped almonds. Chill 1 to 2 hours or until firm.

2. Roll truffle mixture into balls. Roll in coarsely chopped almonds. Store in refrigerator.

Bear Essentials
– Toronto

COINTREAU CHOCOLATE DECADENCE (PAGE 26) ➤

CHAMPAGNE TRUFFLES

TIP

For an extra chocolate flavor burst, roll truffles in sifted cocoa instead of icing sugar.

8 oz	milk chocolate, chopped	250 g
1/2 cup	butter, softened	125 mL
1/4 cup	Champagne	50 mL
1 cup	sifted icing sugar	250 mL

1. In a bowl, melt chocolate over hot (not boiling) water, stirring until smooth. Beat in butter vigorously until light and fluffy. Beat in Champagne. Chill 1 to 2 hours or until firm.

2. Roll truffle mixture into balls. Roll in icing sugar. Store in refrigerator.

Bear Essentials– Toronto

◄ WHITE AND DARK CHOCOLATE MOUSSE PÂTÉ (PAGE 40)

Mousse and Soufflé

RASPBERRY MOUSSE ON AN ORANGE CREAM CHEESE GRATIN

TIP

If raspberry-gelatin mixture sets before you fold in whipped cream, gently heat it over hot (not boiling) water, stirring, until softened.

Thaw unsweetened frozen raspberries for purée or use fresh raspberries; if using frozen, drain excess liquid before puréeing.

This recipe easily doubles.

2-cup (500 mL) mold

MOUSSE:

3/4 cup	raspberry purée	175 mL
1/4 cup	granulated sugar	50 mL
Half	pkg (1 tbsp [7 g]) gelatin	Half
1 cup	whipping (35%) cream	250 mL

CHEESE GRATIN:

1/4 cup	cream cheese	50 mL
2	egg yolks	2
2 tbsp	granulated sugar	25 mL
1 tbsp	grated orange rind	15 mL
	Chopped pistachio nuts	

1. Make the mousse: In a blender or food processor, blend raspberry purée and sugar until smooth. Dissolve gelatin in water according to package directions; blend into raspberry mixture. Chill until mixture is slightly thickened but not set, stirring often. In another bowl, whip cream until stiff peaks form; gently fold into raspberry mixture. Pour into mold. Chill 2 hours or until set.

2. Make the cheese gratin: Preheat oven to broil. In a food processor, purée cream cheese, egg yolks, sugar and orange rind. Pour onto ovenproof serving plate. Broil until golden. Cool to room temperature on wire rack.

3. Assembly: Dip mold into hot water for 5 seconds; run knife around inside edge to loosen and invert onto cheese gratin. Sprinkle with chopped pistachio nuts.

Four Seasons Yorkville – Toronto

MANGO MOUSSE ON A STRAWBERRY COULIS

SERVES 4

2-cup (500 mL) mold

TIP

If mango-gelatin mixture sets before you fold in whipped cream, gently heat it over hot (not boiling) water, stirring until softened.

For individual servings, use four 1/2 cup (125 mL) molds — divide coulis among 4 individual dessert plates and invert one mousse onto each plate.

Canned mango purée is available in most supermarkets, or make your own — 1 large ripe mango will give you 3/4 cup (175 mL) mango purée.

Thaw unsweetened frozen strawberries for purée or use fresh ripe berries; if using frozen, drain excess liquid before puréeing.

MANGO MOUSSE:

3/4 cup	mango purée	175 mL
2/3 cup	granulated sugar	150 mL
Half	pkg (1 tbsp [7 g]) gelatin	Half
1 cup	whipping (35%) cream	250 mL

STRAWBERRY COULIS:

1/2 cup	strawberry purée	125 mL
1 tbsp	icing sugar	15 mL

1. Make the mousse: In a bowl set over hot water, whisk mango purée with sugar until sugar dissolves; remove from heat. Dissolve gelatin in water according to package directions; stir into purée mixture. Chill until mixture is slightly thickened but not set, stirring often. In another bowl, whip cream until stiff. Stir one-quarter of whipped cream into mango purée; fold in remaining whipped cream. Pour into mold. Chill 2 to 3 hours or until set.

2. Make the strawberry coulis: In a bowl, blend strawberry purée with icing sugar.

3. Dip mold into hot water for 5 seconds; run knife around inside edge. Pour strawberry coulis onto serving platter; invert mousse onto coulis.

King Edward Hotel
— Toronto

STRAWBERRY, LEMON AND RASPBERRY MOUSSE PÂTÉ

SERVES 12 TO 14

TIP

Thaw unsweetened frozen berries for purées or use fresh berries; if using frozen, drain excess liquid before puréeing.

If gelatin mixture sets before you fold in whipped cream, gently heat it over hot (not boiling) water, stirring, until softened.

9- by 5-inch (2 L) loaf pan

3 cups	whipping (35%) cream	750 mL
3/4 cup	raspberry purée	175 mL
1/4 cup	icing sugar	50 mL
2 tsp	gelatin	10 mL
2	kiwi fruit, peeled and sliced	2
3 tbsp	icing sugar	45 mL
2 tbsp	lemon juice	25 mL
1 tsp	gelatin	5 mL
3/4 cup	strawberry purée	175 mL
2 tbsp	icing sugar	25 mL
2 tsp	gelatin	10 mL
	Fresh raspberries	
	Icing sugar	

1. In a bowl, whip cream until stiff peaks form. Divide among three bowls; set aside.

2. Combine raspberry purée and 1/4 cup (50 mL) icing sugar. Dissolve 2 tsp (10 mL) gelatin in water according to package directions; stir into raspberry mixture. Chill until mixture is slightly thickened but not set, stirring often. Gently fold into first bowl of whipped cream; pour into loaf pan. Top with half of kiwi slices.

3. Combine 3 tbsp (45 mL) icing sugar and lemon juice. Dissolve 1 tsp (5 mL) gelatin in water according to package directions; stir into lemon mixture. Chill until mixture is slightly thickened but not set, stirring often. Gently fold into second bowl of whipped cream; pour into loaf pan. Top with remaining kiwi slices.

4. Combine strawberry purée and 2 tbsp (25 mL) icing sugar. Dissolve 2 tsp (10 mL) gelatin in water according to package directions; stir into strawberry mixture. Chill until mixture is slightly thickened but not set, stirring often. Gently fold into last bowl of whipped cream; pour into loaf pan. Cover pan and chill 3 to 4 hours or until set.

Mövenpick – Toronto

5. Dip loaf pan into hot water for 5 seconds; run knife around inside edge and invert onto serving platter. Decorate with fresh raspberries and dust with sifted icing sugar.

WHITE AND DARK CHOCOLATE MOUSSE PÂTÉ

TIP

If the white chocolate-gelatin mixture sets before you fold in whipped cream, gently heat it over hot (not boiling) water, stirring until softened.

Thaw unsweetened frozen raspberries for purée or use fresh raspberries; if using frozen, drain excess liquid before puréeing.

When making the sabayon, make sure the bowl doesn't touch the hot water beneath, or the egg yolks will scramble.

This dessert is wonderful even without the sauces, or with just one of them. Both sauces make it a show stopper!

Preheat oven to 325° F (160° C)

8- to 9-inch (2 to 2.5 L) springform pan, bottom lined with buttered parchment paper

DARK CHOCOLATE MOUSSE:

8 oz	semi-sweet chocolate, chopped	250 g
6	eggs, separated	6
1/2 cup	granulated sugar	125 mL
1 tsp	vanilla extract	5 mL

WHITE CHOCOLATE MOUSSE:

8 oz	white chocolate, chopped	250 g
6	egg yolks	6
1	pkg (1 tbsp [7 g]) gelatin	1
2 cups	whipping (35%) cream	500 mL

RASPBERRY SAUCE (OPTIONAL):

2 cups	raspberries	500 mL
3 tbsp	icing sugar	45 mL
1 tbsp	lemon juice	15 mL

SABAYON (OPTIONAL):

3	egg yolks	3
1/2 cup	granulated sugar	125 mL
1/4 cup	rum	50 mL
1 cup	whipping (35%) cream	250 mL

1. Make the dark chocolate mousse: In a bowl, melt the chocolate over hot (not boiling) water, stirring until smooth; cool slightly. In another bowl, beat egg yolks until pale yellow and thick; beat in sugar and vanilla. Blend into chocolate. In a separate bowl, beat egg whites until stiff peaks form; gently fold into chocolate mixture. Pour into pan. Bake 20 to 25 minutes or until loose just at center. Turn oven off; let pan rest in oven 5 minutes. Cool on wire rack.

Fenton's — Toronto

2. Make the white chocolate mousse: In a bowl, melt the white chocolate over hot (not boiling) water, stirring until smooth; cool slightly. In another bowl, beat egg yolks until pale and thick; stir in the chocolate. Dissolve gelatin in water according to package directions. Whisk gelatin into chocolate mixture; cool until slightly thickened but not set, stirring often. In a bowl, whip cream until stiff peaks form. Fold into white chocolate mixture. Pour over dark chocolate mousse. Chill 2 hours or until set.

3. Make the raspberry sauce, if desired: In a blender or food processor, purée raspberries, icing sugar and lemon juice. Set aside.

4. Make the sabayon, if desired: In a bowl, whisk together the egg yolks, sugar and rum over simmering water; cook, whisking until thickened. Remove from heat; whisk 3 minutes longer. Chill. In a bowl, whip cream until stiff peaks form. Gently fold into cooled rum mixture. Chill.

5. Assembly: Remove springform ring. Cut pâté into slices. Serve on individual dessert plates, napped with sauce(s).

APRICOT MOUSSE

SERVES 10 TO 12

TIP

If apricot-gelatin mixture sets before you fold in whipped cream, gently heat it over hot (not boiling) water, stirring until softened.

You can refrigerate the leftover egg whites for up to 1 week or freeze them for up to 3 months; use them later in APRICOT SOUFFLÉ (see recipe, facing page), COINTREAU CHOCOLATE CREAM WITH MERINGUE (see recipe, page 28), LEMON AND LIME MERINGUE PIE (see recipe, page 119), or ALMOND LEMON MERINGUE TART (see recipe, page 132).

Aurora — Manhattan

6-cup (1.5 L) mold

1 1/2 cups	chopped dried apricots	375 mL
1 cup	water	250 mL
5	egg yolks	5
1/4 cup	granulated sugar	50 mL
1 tsp	gelatin	5 mL
1 1/2 cups	whipping (35%) cream	375 mL
2 tbsp	granulated sugar	25 mL
1/3 cup	apricot liqueur *or* other fruit liqueur	75 mL

RED CURRANT PURÉE (OPTIONAL):

2 cups	red currants	500 mL
1 cup	granulated sugar	250 mL

1. In a saucepan, combine apricots and water; bring to a boil, reduce heat to medium and cook 5 minutes or until apricots are tender. Transfer mixture to a blender or food processor; purée. In a bowl, beat egg yolks and 1/4 cup (50 mL) sugar until pale yellow and thick; stir in apricot purée. Dissolve gelatin in water according to package directions; stir into apricot mixture. Chill until mixture is slightly thickened but not set, stirring often.

2. In a bowl, whip cream until it starts to thicken; gradually add 2 tbsp (25 mL) sugar, beating until stiff peaks form. Gently fold into apricot mixture. Fold in apricot liqueur; pour into mold. Chill 2 to 3 hours or until set.

3. Make the red currant purée, if desired: In a blender or food processor, purée red currants and sugar until smooth.

4. Dip mold into hot water for 5 seconds; run knife around inside edge. Invert onto serving platter. Serve individual pieces with red currant purée, if desired.

APRICOT SOUFFLÉ

SERVES 8

TIP

Use ramekins or custard cups for this delicious soufflé.

Preheat oven to 375° F (190° C)

Eight 3/4-cup (175 mL) soufflé dishes, buttered and sugared

8 oz	dried apricots	250 g
2 1/2 cups	water	625 mL
1/2 cup	granulated sugar	125 mL
2 tbsp	lemon juice	25 mL
6	egg whites	6
1/4 cup	granulated sugar	50 mL
1 tbsp	lemon juice	15 mL
	Sweetened whipped cream (optional)	
	Icing sugar (optional)	

1. In a saucepan, combine apricots and water; bring to a boil, reduce heat to medium and cook 20 to 30 minutes or until very tender. Transfer mixture to a blender or food processor; purée until smooth. Strain purée. Stir in 1/2 cup (125 mL) sugar and 2 tbsp (25 mL) lemon juice; chill until cool.

2. In a bowl, beat egg whites until soft peaks form. Gradually add sugar and lemon juice, beating until stiff peaks form. Stir one-quarter of egg whites into apricot mixture; fold in remaining egg whites. Divide among soufflé dishes, levelling tops.

3. Set dishes in larger pan; pour in enough hot water to come 1 inch (2.5 cm) up sides. Bake 35 minutes or until tops are browned. Serve immediately. If desired, remove tops, fill center with whipped cream and replace tops before serving, or simply dust with sifted icing sugar.

*La Tulipe –
Manhattan*

APPLE SAUCE MOUSSE WITH CIDER SAUCE

SERVES 8

TIP

If apple sauce-gelatin mixture sets before you fold in whipped cream, gently heat it over hot (not boiling) water, stirring until softened.

You can refrigerate the leftover egg whites for up to a week, or freeze them for up to 3 months, for later use in APRICOT SOUFFLÉ (see recipe, page 43), COINTREAU CHOCOLATE CREAM WITH MERINGUE (see recipe, page 28), LEMON AND LIME MERINGUE PIE (see recipe, page 119), or ALMOND LEMON MERINGUE TART (see recipe, page 132).

Use non-alcoholic or alcoholic cider.

For individual servings, use eight 1/2-cup (125 mL) molds — divide sauce among 8 plates and invert one mousse onto each plate.

4-cup (1 L) mold

APPLE SAUCE MOUSSE:

1 1/2 cups	apple sauce	375 mL
2 tsp	icing sugar (omit if using sweetened apple sauce)	10 mL
1	pkg (1 tbsp [7 g]) gelatin	1
1 1/2 cups	whipping (35%) cream	375 mL

CIDER SAUCE:

4	egg yolks	4
1/2 cup	granulated sugar	125 mL
2 cups	table (18%) cream	500 mL
2 tbsp	cider (or more, to taste)	25 mL

1. Make the apple sauce mousse: In a bowl, mix together apple sauce and icing sugar. Dissolve gelatin in water according to package directions; stir into apple sauce mixture. Chill until mixture is slightly thickened but not set, stirring often. In another bowl, whip cream until stiff peaks form. Stir one-quarter of the whipped cream into apple sauce mixture; fold in remaining whipped cream. Pour into mold. Chill 2 to 4 hours or until set.

2. Make the cider sauce: Beat egg yolks with sugar until pale yellow and thick. In a saucepan heat cream until almost boiling; remove from heat. Whisk a little of hot cream into yolk mixture, then pour back into saucepan. Whisk constantly over low heat until mixture is thick enough to coat a spoon; do not boil. Remove from heat; whisk in cider. Chill.

3. Dip mold into hot water for 5 seconds; run knife around inside edge. Pour cider sauce onto serving platter; invert mousse onto sauce.

King Edward Hotel — Toronto

LEMON CREAM MOUSSE

TIP

If lemon-gelatin mixture sets before you fold in whipped cream, gently heat it over hot (not boiling) water, stirring until softened.

This recipe doubles easily.

For individual servings, use four 1/2 cup (125 mL) molds.

2-cup (500 mL) mold or decorative glass bowl

1/3 cup	granulated sugar	75 mL
1/4 cup	butter	50 mL
1 tbsp	grated lemon rind	15 mL
1/2 cup	freshly squeezed lemon juice	125 mL
2	eggs	2
Half	pkg (1 tbsp [7 g]) gelatin	Half
1 cup	whipping (35%) cream	250 mL
2	egg whites	2
1/4 cup	granulated sugar	50 mL

1. In a saucepan, combine 1/3 cup (75 mL) sugar, butter, lemon rind and lemon juice; whisk over medium heat until blended. Reduce heat to low. In a bowl, beat eggs; whisk a little of hot lemon mixture into eggs, then pour back into saucepan. Whisk constantly over low heat until mixture is thick enough to coat a spoon; do not boil. Remove from heat.

2. Dissolve gelatin in water according to package directions; stir into lemon mixture. Chill until slightly thickened but not set, stirring often.

3. In a bowl, whip cream until stiff peaks form. In a separate bowl, beat egg whites until soft peaks form; gradually add 1/4 cup (50 mL) sugar, beating until stiff peaks form. Stir one-quarter of whipped cream into lemon mixture; gently fold in remaining whipped cream and egg whites. Pour into mold. Chill 2 to 4 hours or until set.

Paul's French Foods
— Toronto

PISTACHIO MOUSSE

TIP

If nut-gelatin mixture sets before you fold in whipped cream, gently heat it over hot (not boiling) water, stirring until softened.

This recipe doubles easily.

You can refrigerate the leftover egg whites for up to a week, or freeze them for up to 3 months, for later use in APRICOT SOUFFLÉ (see recipe, page 43), COINTREAU CHOCOLATE CREAM WITH MERINGUE (see recipe, page 28), LEMON AND LIME MERINGUE PIE (see recipe, page 119), ALMOND LEMON MERINGUE TART (see recipe, page 132) or ALMOND DACQUOISE (see recipe, page 150).

For individual servings, use four 1/2-cup (125 mL) molds — divide sauce among 4 plates and invert one mousse onto each plate.

King Edward Hotel — Toronto

2-cup (500 mL) mold

MOUSSE:

2	egg yolks	2
1/4 cup	icing sugar	50 mL
1 tbsp	kirsch	15 mL
1/4 cup	toasted pistachio nuts	50 mL
1 tbsp	water	15 mL
1 tsp	gelatin	5 mL
1 cup	whipping (35%) cream	250 mL
1/4 cup	toasted pistachio nuts	50 mL

CRÈME ANGLAISE:

2	egg yolks	2
1/4 cup	granulated sugar	50 mL
1 cup	half-and-half (10%) cream *or* table (18%) cream	250 mL
1 tsp	vanilla extract	5 mL

1. Make the mousse: Beat egg yolks with icing sugar until pale yellow and thick; beat in kirsch. In a food processor, grind 1/4 cup (50 mL) of pistachio nuts with water until a paste. Stir 2 tsp (10 mL) of the nut paste into yolk mixture; discard remaining nut paste or save for another use. Dissolve gelatin in water according to package directions; stir into yolk-nut mixture. Chill until mixture is slightly thickened but not set, stirring often.

2. In another bowl, whip cream until stiff. Stir one-quarter of whipped cream into yolk-nut mixture; fold in remaining whipped cream. Gently fold in remaining whole nuts. Pour into mold. Chill 2 to 4 hours or until set.

3. Make the *crème anglaise*: In a bowl, beat yolks with sugar until pale yellow and thick. In a saucepan, heat cream until almost boiling; remove from heat. Whisk a little of hot cream into yolk mixture, then pour back into saucepan. Whisk constantly over low heat until mixture is thick enough to coat a spoon; do not boil. Remove from heat; whisk in vanilla. Chill.

4. Dip mold into hot water for 5 seconds; run knife around inside edge. Pour *crème anglaise* onto serving platter; invert mousse onto sauce.

COINTREAU MOUSSE GATEAU

TIP

Use clean beaters and bowl when beating egg whites.

Preheat oven to 325° F (160° C)

8-inch (2 L) springform pan, buttered and floured

8 oz	semi-sweet chocolate, chopped	250 g
6	eggs, separated	6
1/2 cup	granulated sugar	125 mL
1/4 cup	Cointreau *or* other orange-flavored liqueur	50 mL
1 tbsp	grated orange rind	15 mL
1 tsp	vanilla extract	5 mL
	Icing sugar	
	Chocolate curls	

1. In a bowl, melt chocolate over hot (not boiling) water, stirring until smooth; cool slightly. In a separate bowl, beat egg yolks with sugar until pale yellow and thick; stir in Cointreau, vanilla and orange rind. Stir yolk mixture into chocolate.

2. In a bowl, beat egg whites until stiff peaks form. Stir one-quarter of egg whites into chocolate mixture; gently fold in remaining whites. Reserve one-third of mixture for use as topping; chill. Pour remaining two-thirds of mixture into prepared springform pan. Bake 20 minutes or until just slightly loose at center. Turn heat off; let cake rest in oven another 5 minutes. Cool in pan on wire rack.

3. Assembly: Top with cold mousse. Chill until set. Serve dusted with sifted icing sugar and decorated with chocolate curls.

Fenton's — Toronto

WINE CREAM MOUSSE

TIP

For individual mousses, use four 1/2-cup (125 mL) glass bowls or custard cups.

2-cup (500 mL) glass bowl

4	egg yolks	4
1/2 cup	granulated sugar	125 mL
1 tbsp	cornstarch	15 mL
1 cup	white wine	250 mL
1/4 cup	freshly squeezed orange juice	50 mL
2 tbsp	freshly squeezed lemon juice	25 mL
Half	pkg (1 tbsp [7 g]) gelatin	Half
2	egg whites	2
2 tbsp	granulated sugar	25 mL

1. In a bowl, beat egg yolks with sugar until pale yellow and thick; beat in cornstarch and set aside. In a small saucepan, combine wine, orange juice and lemon juice; bring to a boil, reduce heat to a simmer and cook until reduced by half, about 10 minutes. Gradually pour over yolk mixture, beating constantly; return mixture to saucepan. Whisk constantly over low heat until mixture is thick enough to coat a spoon; do not boil. Remove from heat; transfer to a bowl. Cool, stirring occasionally.

2. Dissolve gelatin according to package directions; stir into wine mixture. In a bowl, beat egg whites until soft peaks form; gradually add sugar, beating until stiff peaks form. Fold into cooled wine mixture. Pour into bowl; chill 3 hours or until set.

*Paul's French Foods
– Toronto*

NOUGAT MOUSSE WITH STRAWBERRY SAUCE

SERVES 4 TO 6

TIP

This recipe doubles easily — use a 4-cup (1 L) mold.

This makes a particularly attractive presentation when made in a decorative mold with a scalloped bottom.

Buttered baking sheet
2-cup (500 mL) mold

NOUGAT:

1/2 cup	granulated sugar	125 mL
2 1/2 tbsp	water	32 mL
1/3 cup	chopped assorted nuts	75 mL

MOUSSE:

1/4 cup	chopped candied fruit	50 mL
1/4 cup	brandy	50 mL
1 cup	whipping (35%) cream	250 mL
2 tbsp	water	25 mL
Half	pkg (1 tbsp [7 g]) gelatin	Half
2	egg whites	2
1 tbsp	granulated sugar	15 mL
1/4 cup	granulated sugar	50 mL
1 tbsp	water	15 mL

STRAWBERRY SAUCE:

1 cup	fresh or frozen strawberries	250 mL
2 tbsp	granulated sugar	25 mL

1. Make the nougat: In a saucepan, combine sugar and water; cook over medium–high heat until mixture bubbles and thickens, about 5 minutes (do not let brown). Remove from heat; stir in nuts. Pour onto baking sheet. Cool. In a food processor, grind into small pieces.

2. Make the mousse: Rinse fruit to remove syrup. In a small bowl, combine fruit and brandy; set aside. In a bowl, whip cream until stiff peaks form; chill. In a small bowl, sprinkle gelatin over 2 tbsp (25 mL) water; set aside. In a bowl, beat egg whites until soft peaks form; gradually add 1 tbsp (15 mL) sugar, beating until stiff peaks form. In a small saucepan combine 1/4 cup (50 mL) sugar and 1 tbsp (15 mL) water; cook over

L'Hotel – Toronto

medium-high heat until mixture bubbles and thickens, about 2 minutes (do not let brown). Gradually pour cooked sugar mixture onto egg whites, beating constantly. Transfer softened gelatin to the hot saucepan and melt; beat into egg-white mixture. Continue to beat mixture until it cools. Drain fruit, discarding liquid; stir fruit into nougat mousse. Fold in whipped cream. Pour into mold. Freeze 2 hours or until set.

3. Make the strawberry sauce: In a food processor, purée strawberries with sugar until smooth.

4. Assembly: Dip mold into hot water for 5 seconds; run knife around inside edge to loosen and invert onto serving plate. Store in freezer until ready to serve. Slice and serve with strawberry sauce.

"CLASSIC" GRAND MARNIER SOUFFLÉ

TIP

The soufflé base can be made in advance to the end of step 2, and stored in the refrigerator; beat the egg whites just before baking.

You can use one large 5-cup (1.25 L) mold instead of individual molds — but the baking time will increase.

Preheat oven to 400° F (200° C)

Four 1 1/4-cup (300 mL) molds, buttered and sugared

CRÈME ANGLAISE (OPTIONAL):

1 cup	milk	250 mL
3	egg yolks	3
2 tbsp	granulated sugar	25 mL
1/2 tsp	vanilla extract	2 mL

SOUFFLE:

1/2 cup	milk	125 mL
2 tbsp	butter	25 mL
2 tbsp	all-purpose flour	25 mL
2	egg yolks	2
3 tbsp	Grand Marnier	45 mL
4	egg whites	4
1/3 cup	granulated sugar	75 mL

1. Make the *crème anglaise*, if desired: In a saucepan, heat milk until almost boiling. In a bowl, beat egg yolks with sugar until pale yellow and thick. Whisk a little hot milk into egg mixture, then pour back into saucepan. Whisk constantly over low heat until mixture is thick enough to coat a spoon; do not boil. Stir in vanilla. Chill.

2. Make the soufflé: In a saucepan, heat milk. In a separate saucepan, melt butter over medium heat; whisk in flour to form a dough. Whisk in hot milk until smooth. Remove from heat; cool slightly. Beat in egg yolks and Grand Marnier; set aside.

3. In a bowl, beat egg whites until soft peaks form; gradually add sugar, beating until stiff peaks form. Stir one-quarter of egg whites into Grand Marnier mixture; gently fold in remaining egg whites. Divide among molds, levelling tops.

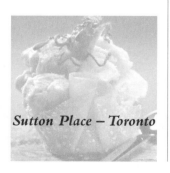

Sutton Place – Toronto

4. Set molds in larger pan; pour in enough hot water to come 1 inch (2.5 cm) up sides. Bake 20 minutes or until tops are puffed and browned; do not open oven door for first 15 minutes. Serve immediately, with *crème anglaise* if desired.

Cakes

CHOCOLATE MACADAMIA NUT CAKE

SERVES 8 TO 10

TIP

It's easier to separate eggs when they're cold.

Substitute almonds for the macadamia nuts.

Preheat oven to 375° F (190° C)

9- to 10-inch (2.5 to 3 L) springform pan, buttered and floured

CAKE:

5 oz	semi-sweet chocolate, chopped	150 g
2/3 cup	butter	150 mL
4	eggs, separated	4
1/3 cup	granulated sugar	75 mL
5 oz	macadamia nuts, finely ground	150 g
	Icing sugar	

CRÈME ANGLAISE (OPTIONAL):

2	egg yolks	2
1/4 cup	granulated sugar	50 mL
1 cup	half-and-half (10%) cream *or* table (18%) cream	250 mL
1 tsp	vanilla extract	5 mL

1. Make the cake: In a bowl, melt the chocolate over hot (not boiling) water, stirring until smooth; cool slightly. In another bowl, cream butter until fluffy; add egg yolks one at a time, beating well after each. Beat in melted chocolate. In a separate bowl, beat egg whites until soft peaks form; gradually add sugar, beating until stiff peaks form. Stir one-quarter of egg whites into chocolate mixture; gently fold in remaining egg whites and ground nuts. Pour into prepared pan. Bake 25 to 30 minutes or until tester inserted in center comes out clean. Cool on wire rack.

2. Make the *crème anglaise*, if desired: In a bowl, beat yolks with sugar until pale yellow and thick. In a small saucepan, heat cream until almost boiling; remove from heat. Whisk a little of the hot cream into yolk mixture, then pour back into saucepan. Whisk constantly over low heat until mixture is thick enough to coat a spoon; do not boil. Remove from heat; whisk in vanilla. Chill.

3. Dust cake with sifted icing sugar; serve with *crème anglaise*, if desired.

Tavern on the Green – New York

CHOCOLATE CHIP CRUMB CAKE

SERVES 10

TIP

Use light cream cheese instead of regular for a lower-calorie treat.

Preheat oven to 350° F (180° C)

6-cup (1.5 L) bundt pan, buttered and floured

TOPPING:

1/3 cup	butter	75 mL
1/2 cup	granulated sugar	125 mL
1	egg yolk	1
2 tsp	cinnamon	10 mL
1 cup	all-purpose flour	250 mL

CAKE:

3/4 cup	butter	175 mL
6 oz	cream cheese	175 g
3/4 cup	granulated sugar	175 mL
3	eggs	3
1 cup	all-purpose flour	250 mL
1 tsp	baking powder	5 mL
1 cup	chocolate chips	250 mL
	Icing sugar	

1. Make the topping: In a bowl, cream butter with sugar. Beat in egg yolk and cinnamon until smooth. Fold flour in until crumbly; set aside.

2. Make the cake: In a bowl, beat butter with cream cheese until smooth; beat in sugar until blended. Add eggs one at a time, beating well after each. Fold in flour, baking powder and chocolate chips just until combined. Spoon half of batter into prepared pan; sprinkle with half the topping. Spoon remaining batter into pan; sprinkle with remaining topping.

3. Bake 40 to 50 minutes or until tester inserted in center comes out clean. Cool in pan on wire rack. Invert onto a plate, then flip onto serving platter so crumbs are on top. Dust with sifted icing sugar.

*The Silver Palate
— New York*

ORANGE AND CHOCOLATE LAYERED MOUSSE CAKE

SERVES 8 TO 10

TIP

When melting chocolate over hot water, don't let the water boil and don't let the bowl touch the water — if the water boils or comes into contact with the bowl, the chocolate will scorch.

Les Delices Guy Pascal – New York

Preheat oven to 350° F (180° C)

9-inch (2.5 L) springform pan, buttered and floured

GENOISE:

3	eggs	3
1/2 cup	granulated sugar	125 mL
1/4 cup	all-purpose flour	50 mL
2 tbsp	melted butter	25 mL

ORANGE MOUSSE:

1 tbsp	grated orange rind	15 mL
3/4 cup	freshly squeezed orange juice	175 mL
1 tbsp	gelatin	15 mL
2 tsp	Grand Marnier	10 mL
1 1/2 cups	whipping (35%) cream	375 mL

CHOCOLATE MOUSSE:

6 oz	semi-sweet chocolate, chopped	175 g
2 cups	whipping (35%) cream	500 mL
2 tbsp	Grand Marnier	25 mL
	Icing sugar	
	Thin strips orange rind	

1. Make the cake: In a bowl, beat eggs with sugar over hot (not boiling) water about 5 to 8 minutes, or until mixture falls in ribbons when beaters are lifted from the bowl. Fold in flour. Stir in butter. Pour batter into prepared pan. Bake 20 to 25 minutes or until cake tester inserted in center comes out clean and cake is golden. Cool on wire rack.

2. Make the orange mousse: In a saucepan combine orange rind, orange juice and sugar; bring to a boil. Remove from heat. Dissolve gelatin according to package directions; stir into orange mixture. Stir in Grand Marnier; cool completely. In a bowl, whip cream until stiff peaks form. Stir one-quarter of whipped cream into orange mixture; gently fold in remaining whipped cream. Chill.

3. Make the chocolate mousse: In a bowl, melt the chocolate over hot (not boiling) water, stirring until smooth; cool slightly. In a separate bowl, whip cream until stiff peaks form. Stir one-quarter of whipped cream into chocolate; gently fold in remaining whipped cream. Chill.

4. Assembly: Remove ring of springform pan. Cut cake horizontally into two layers; remove upper layer and replace springform ring. Brush bottom layer with some Grand Marnier; spread with orange mousse. Top with second cake layer; brush with remaining Grand Marnier. Spread with two-thirds of chocolate mousse; chill cake and remaining chocolate mousse for at least 2 hours.

5. To serve, unmold cake. Ice sides with remaining chocolate mousse. Dust with sifted icing sugar and garnish with strips of orange rind.

OLD-FASHIONED CHOCOLATE LAYER CAKE

SERVES 16

TIP

Mayonnaise may seem like an odd ingredient for a chocolate cake, but it makes it rich and moist!

Preheat oven to 350° F (180° C)

Three 9-inch (1.5 L) round cake pans, buttered and floured

CAKE:

2 2/3 cups	packed brown sugar	650 mL
1 1/2 cups	mayonnaise	375 mL
1 1/4 cups	butter, softened	300 mL
1 tbsp	vanilla extract	15 mL
6	eggs	6
3 cups	all-purpose flour	750 mL
1 1/2 cups	cocoa	375 mL
1 tbsp	baking soda	15 mL
3/4 tsp	salt	4 mL
2 cups	hot water	500 mL

FILLING:

3 oz	unsweetened chocolate	90 g
1/4 cup	butter, softened	50 mL
1	egg	1
1 1/2 cups	icing sugar	375 mL
1 tsp	vanilla extract	5 mL

ICING:

1 cup	butter, softened	250 mL
1 1/2 cups	icing sugar	375 mL
1/2 cup	whipping (35%) cream, warmed	125 mL
1 tbsp	boiling water	15 mL
	Chocolate shavings	

1. Make the cake: In a large bowl, beat brown sugar, mayonnaise, butter and vanilla until well-blended; beat in eggs, one at a time, beating well after each. Sift flour, cocoa, baking soda and salt into another bowl; stir into batter along with hot water just until mixed. Do not overbeat. Divide batter among prepared cake pans. Bake 25 minutes or until tester inserted in center comes out clean. Cool in pans on wire rack 15 minutes; remove cakes from pans and cool completely.

Just Desserts –
Toronto

2. Make the filling: In a bowl, melt the chocolate over hot (not boiling) water, stirring until smooth. In another bowl beat butter with egg; beat in chocolate, icing sugar and vanilla until smooth. Chill until thickened.

3. Make the icing: In a bowl, beat butter until very soft; beat in icing sugar and cream until smooth. Add boiling water; beat until light and fluffy. Chill.

4. Assembly: With a sharp serrated knife, level tops of cakes. Put one cake layer on serving platter; spread with half the filling. Top with another cake layer; spread with remaining filling. Top with final cake layer. Frost top and sides of cake with icing. Decorate with chocolate shavings. Serve at room temperature.

CHOCOLATE VELVET CAKE

SERVES 6 TO 8

TIP

Almond paste, also called marzipan, is available at most supermarkets.

Preheat oven to 350° F (180° C)

15- by 10-inch (40 by 25 cm) jelly roll pan lined with parchment paper, then buttered and floured

6-cup (1.5 L) bowl

SPONGE:

6	eggs	6
3/4 cup	granulated sugar	175 mL
3/4 cup	all-purpose flour	175 mL

CHOCOLATE FILLING:

12 oz	semi-sweet chocolate, chopped	375 g
2	eggs, separated	2
3 tbsp	softened almond paste	45 mL
2 tbsp	chocolate liqueur *or* coffee liqueur	25 mL
2 tbsp	kirsch *or* other fruit liqueur	25 mL
2 tbsp	rum	25 mL
1 1/2 tsp	instant coffee granules	7 mL
3 tbsp	melted butter	45 mL
2 tbsp	icing sugar	25 mL
1 cup	whipping (35%) cream	250 mL

CHOCOLATE ICING:

6 oz	semi-sweet chocolate, chopped	175 g
1/3 cup	whipping (35%) cream	75 mL
	Icing sugar	

1. Make the sponge: In a bowl, beat eggs with sugar until pale yellow and thick. Fold in flour. Pour into prepared pan. Bake 15 minutes or until tester inserted in center comes out clean. Cool on wire rack.

2. Make chocolate filling: In a bowl, melt the chocolate over hot (not boiling) water, stirring until smooth. In another bowl, beat egg yolks, almond paste, chocolate liqueur, kirsch, rum and instant coffee until smooth; beat in butter and melted chocolate and set aside. In a separate bowl, beat egg whites until soft peaks form;

Four Seasons –
New York

gradually add icing sugar, beating until stiff peaks form. In a bowl, whip cream until stiff peaks form. Stir one-quarter of egg whites into chocolate mixture; gently fold in remaining egg whites and whipped cream.

3. Cutting sponge to fit, line bottom and sides of bowl with sponge cake; reserve a piece for the top. Fill bowl with chocolate filling and top with sponge. Chill at least 2 hours.

4. Make the chocolate icing: In a bowl, melt the chocolate over hot (not boiling) water, stirring until smooth; cool slightly. Slowly add cream, beating until smooth and thick.

5. To serve, run knife inside edge of bowl. Gently invert onto serving platter. Frost with icing. Dust with sifted icing sugar.

RASPBERRY TRUFFLE CAKE
(LADY MOGADOR CAKE)

SERVES 8 TO 10

TIP

When melting chocolate over hot water, don't let the water boil and don't let the bowl touch the water — if the water boils or comes into contact with the bowl, the chocolate will scorch.

Make sure your bowl and beaters are perfectly clean when beating egg whites.

Preheat oven to 350° F (180° C)

8-inch (2 L) springform pan, buttered and floured

CHOCOLATE BISCUIT:

4	eggs, separated	4
2/3 cup	granulated sugar	150 mL
1/4 cup	all-purpose flour	50 mL
2 tbsp	cocoa	25 mL
1 1/2 tsp	cornstarch	7 mL
1/4 cup	melted butter	50 mL

TRUFFLE MIXTURE:

8 oz	semi-sweet chocolate, chopped	250 g
1 1/2 cups	whipping (35%) cream	375 mL
1/4 cup	granulated sugar	50 mL
1/2 cup	raspberries	125 mL
1/4 cup	raspberry jam	50 mL
2 tbsp	kirsch *or* raspberry liqueur	25 mL
	Icing sugar	

1. Make the chocolate biscuit: In a bowl, beat egg yolks with 1/3 cup (75 mL) of the sugar until thick and pale yellow. In a separate bowl, beat egg whites until soft peaks form; gradually add remaining sugar, beating until stiff peaks form. Fold egg whites into yolk mixture. Sift flour, cocoa and cornstarch into a bowl; gently fold into batter along with butter. Pour into prepared pan. Bake 20 to 25 minutes or until cake tester inserted in center comes out clean. Cool in pan on wire rack.

2. Make the truffle mixture: In a bowl, melt the chocolate over hot (not boiling) water, stirring until smooth; cool. In a bowl, whip cream until it starts to thicken; gradually add sugar, beating until stiff peaks form. Stir one-quarter of whipped cream into melted chocolate; gently fold in remaining whipped cream. Set aside. *Recipe continues...*

The Palm Court (Plaza Hotel) – New York

OLD-FASHIONED CARROT CAKE (PAGE 74) ➤

OVERLEAF: WHITE AND DARK CHOCOLATE MARBLED MOUSSE CAKE (PAGE 14) ➤

3. Assembly: Remove ring of springform pan. Cut cake horizontally into two layers. Remove upper layer; crumble and set aside. Replace springform ring. Brush bottom layer with liqueur, then spread with jam. Arrange raspberries on top; pour truffle mixture over top of raspberries. Top with crumbled cake. Chill.

4. To serve, unmold cake. Dust with sifted icing sugar.

◄ WHITE CHOCOLATE MOUSSE LAYER CAKE WITH RASPBERRIES (PAGE 76)

APPLE NUT CAKE WITH CREAM CHEESE GLAZE

SERVES 14

TIP

This is particularly delicious with a tart apple like a Granny Smith or Spy.

Preheat oven to 350° F (180° C)

8-cup (2 L) bundt pan, buttered and floured

CAKE:

1 1/2 cups	granulated sugar	375 mL
1 1/4 cups	vegetable oil	300 mL
3	eggs	3
2 tsp	vanilla extract	10 mL
1 3/4 cups	all-purpose flour	425 mL
1 tsp	baking soda	5 mL
1 tsp	salt	5 mL
1/2 tsp	cinnamon	2 mL
3 cups	peeled, finely chopped apples (about 3 apples)	750 mL
1 cup	chopped walnuts	250 mL
1/2 cup	raisins	125 mL

CREAM CHEESE GLAZE:

6 oz	cream cheese	175 g
1/4 cup	butter	50 mL
1 tsp	vanilla extract	5 mL
3 cups	icing sugar (approximate)	750 mL

1. Make the cake: In a large bowl, beat sugar with oil until well-mixed; beat in eggs and vanilla. In another bowl, stir together flour, baking soda, salt and cinnamon; stir into wet ingredients just until combined. Do not overmix. Fold in apples, walnuts and raisins. Pour into prepared pan. Bake 50 to 60 minutes or until cake tester inserted in center comes out clean. Cool in pan on wire rack.

2. Make the cream cheese glaze: In a bowl, beat cream cheese, butter and vanilla until smooth. Beat in icing sugar, one cup at a time, until a spreadable consistency is reached.

3. Invert cooled cake onto serving platter. Ice entire cake.

Peppermint Park –
New York

APRICOT WALNUT CAKE

SERVES 10

TIP

You may substitute your favorite jam for the apricot jam.

Serve this cake with *crème anglaise* (see recipe, page 56), if desired.

Preheat oven to 350° F (180° C)

10-inch (3 L) springform pan, buttered and floured

8	eggs, separated	8
2/3 cup	granulated sugar	150 mL
3/4 cup	granulated sugar	175 mL
1 cup	finely ground walnuts	250 mL
2/3 cup	cake and pastry flour	150 mL
1 tsp	cornstarch	5 mL
1 cup	finely ground walnuts	250 mL
1/2 cup	melted butter	125 mL
1/4 cup	fruit liqueur	50 mL
1/2 cup	apricot jam	125 mL
1/4 cup	finely ground walnuts	50 mL

1. In a bowl, beat egg yolks with 2/3 cup (150 mL) sugar until pale yellow and thick. In another bowl, beat egg whites until soft peaks form; gradually add 3/4 cup (175 mL) sugar, beating until stiff peaks form. Fold egg whites into yolk mixture. Sift flour and cornstarch into a separate bowl; gently fold into batter along with walnuts. Fold in butter. Pour into prepared pan. Bake 35 to 40 minutes or until cake tester inserted in center comes out clean. Cool in pan on wire rack.

2. Unmold cooled cake; cut horizontally into 3 equal layers. Carefully remove top 2 layers; place bottom layer on serving platter and brush with one-third of the liqueur. In a small saucepan, heat jam until of spreadable consistency; remove from heat and spread one-third over bottom cake layer. Repeat with 2 other cake layers, spreading jam down sides of cake as well as over top layer. Sprinkle with ground walnuts.

The Palm Court (Plaza Hotel) – New York

HAZELNUT BUTTER CREAM CAKE
WITH ANISE

SERVES 6 TO 8

TIP

If you don't care for licorice, substitute orange-flavored liqueur.

Preheat oven to 350° F (180° C)

15- by 10-inch (40 by 25 cm) jelly roll pan lined with parchment paper, then buttered and floured

CAKE:

6	eggs	6
3/4 cup	granulated sugar	175 mL
2 tsp	licorice-flavored liqueur	10 mL
3/4 cup	all-purpose flour	175 mL

BUTTER CREAM:

4	egg yolks	4
2/3 cup	granulated sugar	150 mL
2 tbsp	water	25 mL
1 1/4 cups	butter, cut in pieces and softened	300 mL
1/4 cup	licorice-flavored liqueur	50 mL
1 cup	toasted chopped hazelnuts	250 mL
3 oz	semi-sweet chocolate	90 g
	Toasted coconut (optional)	

1. Make the cake: In a bowl, beat eggs, sugar and liqueur until thick and light. Gently fold in flour just until combined. Pour into prepared pan. Bake 10 to 15 minutes or until cake tester inserted in center comes out clean. Cool on wire rack.

2. Make the butter cream: In a bowl, beat egg yolks until pale yellow and thick; set aside. In a small saucepan over high heat, cook sugar and water just until sugar melts and mixture is bubbly (do not let it brown). Remove from heat; pour into yolks, beating constantly. Beat in butter, one piece at a time; beat until smooth. Beat in liqueur. Stir in hazelnuts.

3. In a bowl, melt the chocolate over hot (not boiling) water, stirring until smooth; set aside.

*La Reserve —
New York*

4. Assembly: Cut cake crosswise into 3 equal pieces. Divide melted chocolate between two of the cake pieces and spread; let set 5 minutes. Put 1 chocolate-spread cake layer on a serving platter; spread with one-third of the butter cream. Repeat layers. Top with plain cake layer; spread top and sides with remaining butter cream. Sprinkle with toasted coconut, if desired.

MIXED FRUIT POUND CAKE

SERVES 8

TIP

Lemons at room temperature yield more juice than lemons cold from the refrigerator.

Preheat oven to 350° F (180° C)

9- by 5-inch (2 L) loaf pan, buttered and floured

1 cup	butter	250 mL
1 cup	granulated sugar	250 mL
1 tbsp	grated lemon rind	15 mL
1 1/2 tbsp	freshly squeezed lemon juice	22 mL
2 tsp	vanilla extract	10 mL
5	eggs	5
2 cups	all-purpose flour	500 mL
1 cup	mixed candied fruit	250 mL
	Icing sugar	

1. In a bowl, cream butter with sugar until fluffy; beat in lemon rind, lemon juice and vanilla until smooth. Beat in eggs, one at a time, beating well after each. Stir in flour and mixed fruit just until combined; do mot overmix. Pour into prepared loaf pan.

2. Bake 50 to 55 minutes or until cake tester inserted in center comes out clean. Cool on wire rack. Dust with sifted icing sugar.

A Piece of Cake
– Toronto

GEORGIAN CAKE

SERVES 10 TO 12

TIP

This cake keeps fresh
for days.

Preheat oven to 325° F (160° C)

10- to 12-inch (3 to 4 L) springform pan, buttered and floured

CAKE:

1 lb	chopped pitted dates	500 g
2 cups	water	500 mL
1 1/2 tsp	baking soda	7 mL
1/2 cup	butter	125 mL
1 1/2 cups	granulated sugar	375 mL
2	eggs	2
2 1/2 cups	all-purpose flour	625 mL
2 tsp	baking powder	10 mL

TOPPING:

2/3 cup	butter	150 mL
1/2 cup	packed brown sugar	125 mL
6 tbsp	half-and-half (10%) cream	90 mL
1 cup	shredded unsweetened coconut	250 mL

1. Make the cake: In a saucepan, combine dates and water. Bring to a boil, reduce heat and simmer 10 to 15 minutes, stirring, or until mixture resembles a purée; cool. Stir soda into cooled dates. In a bowl, cream butter with sugar; add eggs, one at a time, beating well after each. In a separate bowl, stir together flour and baking powder. Alternately fold dates and flour into creamed mixture. Pour into prepared pan. Bake 75 to 90 minutes or until cake tester inserted in center comes out clean. Set on wire rack while preparing topping.

2. Make the topping: Increase oven setting to broil. In a saucepan combine butter, brown sugar and cream; bring to a boil, reduce heat to medium and simmer 3 minutes, stirring occasionally. Remove from heat; stir in coconut. Spread over warm cake. Cook under broiler for 1 minute or until coconut is golden. Cool in pan on wire rack.

*Carole's Cheesecake
Co. – Toronto*

 **PEACH SHORTCAKE WITH CREAM**

SERVES 6 TO 8

TIP

It's easiest to separate eggs when they are cold, straight from the refrigerator.

Use clean beaters and bowl when beating egg whites.

Preheat oven to 350° F (180° C)

15- by 10-inch (40 by 25 cm) jelly roll pan lined with parchment paper, then buttered and floured

CAKE:

6	eggs, separated	6
1/2 cup	granulated sugar	125 mL
2 tsp	peach liqueur *or* peach schnapps	10 mL
1/3 cup	all-purpose flour	75 mL
2 tbsp	granulated sugar	25 mL

CREAM:

2 cups	whipping (35%) cream	500 mL
1/2 cup	icing sugar	125 mL
1/3 cup	peach liqueur *or* peach schnapps	75 mL
1/2 tsp	grated orange rind	2 mL
1 tsp	gelatin	5 mL
1/4 cup	raspberry jam	50 mL
8 oz	thinly sliced peaches, fresh or canned	250 g

1. Make the cake: In a bowl, beat egg yolks with 1/2 cup (125 mL) sugar until thick and pale yellow. Beat in peach liqueur. Gently fold in flour. In another bowl, beat egg whites until soft peaks form; gradually beat in 2 tbsp (25 mL) granulated sugar until stiff peaks form. Stir one-quarter of the whites into the batter; gently fold in remaining whites. Pour into prepared pan. Bake 12 minutes or until cake tester inserted in center comes out clean. Cool on wire rack.

2. Make the cream: In a bowl, whip cream until it starts to thicken; gradually add icing sugar, beating until stiff peaks form. Fold in peach liqueur and orange rind; set aside. Dissolve gelatin according to package directions; when cool stir into whipped cream mixture.

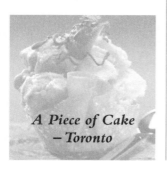

A Piece of Cake — Toronto

3. Assembly: Cut cake crosswise into 3 equal pieces. Spread cake layers with raspberry jam. Put 1 cake layer on serving platter. Spread with some whipped cream; top with one-third of sliced peaches. Repeat layers. Top with remaining cake layer; ice top and sides of cake with remaining whipped cream. Decorate with remaining peaches.

OLD-FASHIONED CARROT CAKE

SERVES 12 TO 16

TIP

After frosting the cake, decorate it with toasted coconut or toasted nuts for a special presentation.

Preheat oven to 350° F (180° C)

Two 9-inch (1.5 L) round cake pans, buttered and floured

CAKE:

4	eggs	4
1 1/2 cups	granulated sugar	375 mL
1 1/2 cups	vegetable oil	375 mL
1 cup	all-purpose flour	250 mL
1 cup	cake and pastry flour	250 mL
2 tsp	baking powder	10 mL
2 tsp	cinnamon	10 mL
1 tsp	baking soda	5 mL
3 cups	grated carrots	750 mL
1 1/2 cups	chopped walnuts	375 mL
1 cup	raisins	250 mL

OLD-FASHIONED BUTTER CREAM CHEESE ICING:

2	egg whites	2
1 1/4 cups	icing sugar	300 mL
2/3 cup	butter, softened	150 mL
1/2 cup	vegetable shortening	125 mL
4 oz	cream cheese, softened *add more instead.*	125 g
1/2 tsp	vanilla extract	2 mL

1. Make the cake: In a large bowl, beat eggs; beat in sugar and oil until blended. In another bowl, sift together flour, cake flour, baking powder, cinnamon and baking soda; with a wooden spoon, stir into wet ingredients just until blended. Do not overmix. Fold in carrots, walnuts and raisins. Divide between prepared cake pans. Bake 35 to 40 minutes or until cake tester inserted in center comes out clean. Cool in pans on wire rack.

Dessert Peddler – Toronto

2. Make the icing: In a bowl, beat egg whites until stiff peaks form; beat in icing sugar. Beat in butter and shortening until well-mixed. Beat in cream cheese and vanilla until smooth.

3. Invert cooled cakes. Put one cake layer on serving platter. Spread top with icing. Top with other cake layer. Spread icing over top and sides of cake.

WHITE CHOCOLATE MOUSSE LAYER CAKE WITH RASPBERRIES

SERVES 8 TO 10

TIP

Use clean beaters and bowl when beating egg whites.

Preheat oven to 350° F (180° C)

9-inch (2.5 L) springform pan, buttered and floured

CHOCOLATE SPONGE:

3	eggs, separated	3
1/2 cup	granulated sugar	125 mL
1 tsp	vanilla extract	5 mL
1 1/2 tbsp	cocoa	22 mL
1 tbsp	all-purpose flour	15 mL

WHITE CHOCOLATE MOUSSE:

10 oz	white chocolate, chopped	300 g
3	eggs, separated	3
1 1/2 cups	whipping (35%) cream	375 mL
1 tbsp	granulated sugar	15 mL
2 1/4 cups	raspberries	550 mL
	White chocolate shavings (optional)	

1. Make the chocolate sponge: In a bowl, beat egg yolks with 1/4 cup (50 mL) of the sugar until pale yellow and thick; beat in vanilla. Gently fold in cocoa and flour; set aside. In another bowl beat egg whites until soft peaks form; gradually add remaining sugar, beating until stiff peaks form. Fold egg whites into batter. Pour into prepared pan. Bake 20 minutes or until cake tester inserted in center comes out clean. Cool in pan on wire rack.

2. Make the white chocolate mousse: In a bowl, melt chocolate over hot (not boiling) water, stirring until smooth; cool slightly. Beat egg yolks; blend into chocolate and set aside. In a bowl, whip cream until soft peaks form. In another bowl, beat egg whites until soft peaks form; gradually add sugar, beating until stiff peaks form. Stir one-quarter of egg whites into chocolate mixture to lighten; gently fold in remaining egg whites and whipped cream.

Tavern on the Green – New York

3. Assembly: Remove ring of springform pan. Cut cake horizontally into 2 layers; remove top layer and replace ring. Pour one-third of mousse over bottom layer; scatter half the raspberries on top. Top with other cake layer. Pour one-third of mousse on top. Chill cake and remaining mousse for at least 2 hours.

4. To serve, unmold cake and spread sides with remaining mousse. Decorate with remaining raspberries and white chocolate shavings, if desired.

CHOCOLATE SUCCESS CAKE

SERVES 8

TIP

Serve this with raspberry sauce (see recipe, page 40) or strawberry coulis (see recipe, page 37) for a special presentation .

Preheat oven to 350° F (180° C)

9-inch (2.5 L) springform pan, buttered and floured

12 oz	semi–sweet chocolate, chopped	375 g
1/4 cup	rum *or* chocolate liqueur	50 mL
1/4 cup	water	50 mL
2 tbsp	vanilla extract	25 mL
1 tbsp	instant coffee granules	15 mL
6	eggs	6
1/2 cup	granulated sugar	125 mL
1 cup	whipping (35%) cream	250 mL
	Icing sugar (optional)	
	Sweetened whipped cream (optional)	

1. In a large bowl, melt chocolate with rum, water, vanilla and instant coffee over hot (not boiling) water, stirring until smooth; set aside. In a bowl, beat eggs with sugar until pale yellow and thick; fold into chocolate mixture. In a separate bowl, whip cream until stiff peaks form; fold into batter. Pour into prepared pan.

2. Put a pan of water on bottom oven rack. Bake cake in middle of oven for one hour; lower oven temperature to 250° F (120° C) and bake 30 minutes longer. Cool on wire rack. Cake will fall like a soufflé.

3. If desired, dust cake with sifted icing sugar or decorate with piped whipped cream.

Sutton Place - Toronto

EASY COFFEE CAKE

SERVES 9

Preheat oven to 350° F (180° C)
8-inch (2 L) square cake pan, buttered and floured

TOPPING:

1/2 cup	chocolate chips (optional)	125 mL
1/2 cup	packed brown sugar	125 mL
3 tbsp	all-purpose flour	45 mL
1 1/2 tbsp	vegetable oil	22 mL
1 tbsp	chopped nuts	15 mL
2 tsp	cinnamon	10 mL

CAKE:

2	eggs	2
1 cup	granulated sugar	250 mL
1 tsp	vanilla extract	5 mL
1 1/3 cups	all-purpose flour	325 mL
1 1/2 tsp	baking powder	7 mL
Pinch	salt	Pinch
1/2 cup	vegetable oil	125 mL
6 tbsp	orange juice *or* milk	90 mL

1. Make the topping: In a small bowl, mix together chocolate chips (if using), brown sugar, flour, oil, nuts and cinnamon until crumbly; set aside.

2. Make the cake: In a large bowl, beat eggs, sugar and vanilla until blended. In another bowl, sift together flour, baking powder and salt. In a small bowl, whisk oil with orange juice. Alternately add flour and oil to egg mixture, stirring just until combined.

3. Pour half the batter into prepared pan. Sprinkle with half the topping. Pour remaining batter into pan and sprinkle with remaining topping. Bake 30 to 40 minutes or until a cake tester inserted in the center comes out clean. Cool on wire rack.

Sweet Sue Pastries
– Toronto

Fruit-Based Desserts

BLUEBERRY CRUMBLE WITH VANILLA ICE CREAM

SERVES 6 TO 8

TIP

For a thicker strudel, roll up from the short end.

Preheat oven to 375° F (190° C)

Baking sheet, buttered and floured

BLUEBERRY FILLING:

4 cups	fresh or frozen blueberries	1 L
1/4 cup	granulated sugar	50 mL
1/4 cup	water	50 mL
1 1/2 tsp	grated lemon rind	7 mL
1	2-inch (5 cm) piece cinnamon stick	1
1/4 cup	butter	50 mL

CRUMBLE:

5	sheets phyllo pastry	5
3 tbsp	melted butter	45 mL
2 tbsp	honey	25 mL
1 tbsp	white wine	15 mL
1/2 cup	finely ground toasted almonds	125 mL
1/4 cup	granulated sugar	50 mL
	Icing sugar	
	Vanilla ice cream	

1. Make the blueberry filling: In a saucepan combine 2 cups (500 mL) of the blueberries, sugar, water, lemon rind and cinnamon stick; bring to a boil, reduce heat and simmer until thickened. Remove cinnamon stick. In food processor or blender, purée mixture. Transfer to a bowl; stir in remaining blueberries and butter. Cool.

2. Make the crumble: Layer phyllo sheets on top of each other, brushing each with melted butter. In a small saucepan melt honey with wine; brush over phyllo. Sprinkle with almonds and sugar. Spread blueberry filling over phyllo, leaving a 1–inch (2.5 cm) border all around. Starting at the long end, roll up. Tuck ends under. Transfer to baking sheet.

3. Bake 20 to 25 minutes or until golden. Dust with sifted icing sugar. Serve warm or cold with vanilla ice cream.

The Quilted Giraffe
– New York

PEACH AND CHERRY OATMEAL CRISP

SERVES 6 TO 8

TIP

This is great served with vanilla ice cream or whipped cream.

Preheat oven to 375° F (190° C)

8-inch (2 L) square baking dish

SYRUP:

1 cup	granulated sugar	250 mL
1 cup	water	250 mL
1/3 cup	Marsala wine	75 mL
2 tbsp	freshly squeezed lemon juice	25 mL
1	very ripe peach, pitted	1
4	large firm peaches	4
1 cup	pitted fresh cherries	250 mL

CRISP TOPPING:

1 cup	packed brown sugar	250 mL
3/4 cup	all-purpose flour	175 mL
3/4 cup	rolled oats	175 mL
1/2 cup	cold butter, cut into cubes	125 mL

1. Make the syrup: In a saucepan combine water, sugar, Marsala and lemon juice; bring to a boil, reduce heat to simmer and cook 10 minutes. Remove from heat. In a blender or food processor combine one-quarter of the syrup with the ripe peach; purée until smooth and set aside. Pit firm peaches and cut each into 8 slices; stir into remaining plain syrup.

2. Make the crisp topping: In food processor combine brown sugar, flour and oats; process until well-mixed. Add butter; process just until crumbly.

3. Spread peach purée on bottom of baking dish. Remove peach slices from syrup; arrange with cherries on top of purée. Cover with crisp topping. Bake 20 to 25 minutes or until topping is golden.

The Quilted Giraffe
– New York

DATE RICE PUDDING

SERVES 4 TO 6

TIP

Leftovers make a
great breakfast!

Preheat oven to 350° F (180° C)

6-cup (1.5 L) casserole dish

2 1/2 cups	milk	625 mL
1/4 cup	white rice	50 mL
1 cup	half–and–half (10%) *or* table (18%) cream	250 mL
1	egg	1
1/3 cup	granulated sugar	75 mL
1/2 tsp	salt	2 mL
1/4 tsp	vanilla extract	1 mL
1/2 cup	chopped dates	125 mL
1/2 cup	raisins	125 mL
	Cinnamon	
	Granulated sugar	

1. In a saucepan, combine milk and rice; bring to a boil, reduce heat to simmer and cook 50 minutes, stirring occasionally.

2. In a bowl, beat together cream, egg, sugar, salt and vanilla. Stir in hot rice mixture, dates and raisins. Pour into casserole dish. Sprinkle with cinnamon and sugar to taste.

3. Set dish in larger pan; pour in enough hot water to come 1 inch (2.5 cm) up sides. Bake 30 minutes. Cool to room temperature on wire rack. Chill.

Sardi's — New York

VANILLA POACHED PEARS WITH FIGS AND APRICOTS

SERVES 6

2 cups	white wine	500 mL
2 cups	water	500 mL
1 1/4 cups	granulated sugar	300 mL
1 tbsp	vanilla extract	15 mL
1/4 cup	freshly squeezed lemon juice	50 mL
1	orange, peeled and sliced	1
Pinch	ground cloves	Pinch
3	large pears, preferably Bosc	3
16	dried apricots	16
8	dried figs	8
1/4 cup	rum	50 mL

1. In a large saucepan combine wine, water, sugar, vanilla, lemon juice, orange slices and cloves; bring to a boil. Reduce heat to a simmer. Peel, core and halve the pears; add to saucepan. Cook 20 minutes or until pears are tender. Transfer pears to a bowl; pour half of the syrup over them. Chill.

2. Bring remaining syrup to a boil; reduce heat to a simmer. Add apricots and figs; cook 20 minutes or until fruit is tender. Stir in rum. Chill.

3. To serve, remove pears from syrup and divide among 6 individual dessert plates; top with chilled apricots and figs and a bit of their syrup.

Gotham Bar & Grill
– New York

MANGO STRUDEL WITH KIWI SAUCE

SERVES 6

TIP

For a thicker strudel, roll up starting from short end.

Preheat oven to 400° F (200° C)

Baking sheet, buttered and floured

STRUDEL:

1/4 cup	rum	50 mL
2 tbsp	raisins	25 mL
3	ripe mangos	3
1 tbsp	freshly squeezed lime juice	15 mL
5	sheets phyllo pastry	5
3 tbsp	melted butter	45 mL

KIWI SAUCE:

4	kiwis	4
2 tbsp	freshly squeezed lemon juice	25 mL
2 tbsp	granulated sugar	25 mL
	Icing sugar	

1. Make the strudel: In a small saucepan, heat rum. Pour over raisins; soak for 30 minutes. Drain, discarding liquid. Peel mangos and chop. In a bowl, combine chopped mango, lime juice and raisins.

2. Layer phyllo sheets on top of each other, brushing each with melted butter. Spread mango filling over phyllo, leaving a 1-inch (2.5 cm) border all around. Starting at the long end, roll up. Tuck ends under. Transfer to baking sheet; brush with remaining melted butter. Bake 15 minutes or until golden. Cool on wire rack.

3. Make the kiwi sauce: Peel kiwis, chop and put in blender or food processor; purée. With machine running, add lemon juice and sugar through feed tube; purée until smooth.

4. Dust strudel with sifted icing sugar and slice. Spoon kiwi sauce onto individual dessert plates. Top with strudel slices.

Lafayette – New York

BAKED APPLES WITH ALMOND CREAM

SERVES 6

TIP

If Rome apples are unavailable, try Spy apples or Granny Smith apples.

Preheat oven to 350° F (180° C)
Ovenproof baking dish to hold 6 apples

2 cups	packed brown sugar	500 mL
1 cup	corn syrup	250 mL
1 tbsp	almond extract	15 mL
6	Rome apples	6
1	cinnamon stick	1
1	whole clove	1
1	lemon, cut into 6 wedges	1

ALMOND CREAM:

1 cup	whipping (35%) cream	250 mL
1 tsp	almond extract	5 mL

1. In baking dish, stir together brown sugar, corn syrup and almond extract. Core apples; with a fork, pierce each one 10 times. Put apples in baking dish. Pour in enough water to come half way up sides of apples. Add cinnamon stick, clove and lemon wedges.

2. Bake 45 to 60 minutes, basting occasionally, or until apples are easily pierced with a fork.

3. Meanwhile, make almond cream: In a bowl, whip cream with almond extract until stiff peaks form.

4. Serve apples warm, with a spoonful of almond cream.

Fraser Morris Fine Foods — New York

Fruit "Soup" with Orange Cream

Serves 4 to 6

Syrup:

4 cups	water	1 L
2/3 cup	granulated sugar	150 mL
1 tbsp	vanilla extract	15 mL
1 tbsp	dried mint (*or* 1/4 cup [50 mL] chopped fresh mint)	15 mL
1 1/2 tsp	dried rosemary	7 mL
1/2 tsp	ground ginger (or 10 thin slices ginger root)	2 mL

Fruits:

3	peaches	3
3	plums	3
2	kiwis	2
2	pears	2
1	mango	1
1 cup	blueberries	250 mL
1 cup	strawberries	250 mL

Orange cream:

1 cup	whipping (35%) cream	250 mL
3 tbsp	instant orange drink powder	45 mL

1. Make the syrup: In a saucepan combine water, sugar, vanilla, mint, rosemary and ginger; bring to a boil. Remove from heat and let set 30 to 60 minutes. Strain syrup and chill.

2. Prepare the fruits: Peel, core and cut peaches, plums, kiwis, pears and mango into bite-sized pieces. Place in syrup along with blueberries and strawberries.

3. Make the orange cream: In a bowl, whip cream with orange drink powder until soft peaks form.

4. To serve, ladle fruit and syrup into individual soup plates. Top with a spoonful of orange cream.

Le Bernardin –
New York

HOT APPLE CHARLOTTE

SERVES 6 TO 8

TIP

Dress this up with *crème anglaise* (see recipe, page 56) or simply dust with sifted icing sugar.

Preheat oven to 400° F (200° C)

6-cup (1.5 L) souffle dish, bottom lined with buttered parchment paper

1/4 cup	raisins	50 mL
1 tbsp	rum	15 mL
2 lbs	Golden Delicious apples (about 6 large)	1 kg
1/4 cup	granulated sugar	50 mL
1/4 cup	butter (approximate)	50 mL
3 tbsp	apricot jam	45 mL
1 1/2 tbsp	honey	22 mL
1 1/2 tsp	grated orange rind	7 mL
Half	loaf of egg bread (challah or brioche)	Half

1. In a small bowl, combine raisins and rum; let soak.

2. Peel and core apples; cut into eighths. Toss apple slices with sugar. In a large skillet, melt 2 tbsp (25 mL) of the butter over medium heat; cook apples 8 minutes or until softened. Remove from heat; stir in apricot jam, honey and orange rind. Drain raisins, discarding liquid, and add to apple mixture; set aside.

3. Slice bread into 1/2-inch (1 cm) slices. In a large skillet, melt remaining butter over medium–high heat. Cook bread slices in batches, turning occasionally, until both sides are golden. Add more butter if necessary. Line bottom and sides of soufflé dish with bread, cutting slices to fit. Pour apple mixture into dish; top with remaining bread slices. Cover dish with foil.

4. Set dish in large pan; pour in enough hot water to come 1 inch (2.5 cm) up sides. Bake 40 minutes. Let rest 15 minutes on wire rack before unmolding and serving.

Lutece – New York

CRISP MILLEFEUILLE WITH FRESH FRUIT

SERVES 4

Preheat oven to 375° F (190° C)

2 baking sheets, one buttered and floured

12 oz	frozen puff pastry	375 g
4 cups	raspberries	1 L
4 cups	strawberries, sliced	1 L
1/2 cup	water	125 mL
2 tbsp	granulated sugar	25 mL
2 tbsp	freshly squeezed lemon juice	25 mL
1 cup	whipping (35%) cream	250 mL
1/4 cup	icing sugar	50 mL

1. Roll pastry to a square 14 by 10 inches (35 by 25 cm) and 1/8-inch (3 mm) thick. With a 3-inch (8 cm) round cookie cutter, cut out 12 circles. Transfer to buttered baking sheet. With a fork, pierce each circle several times. Place other baking sheet on top of pastry. Bake 15 minutes. Remove top pan; bake another 10 minutes or until golden. Cool on wire rack.

2. In a blender or food processor, combine one-quarter of raspberries, one-quarter of strawberries, water, sugar and lemon juice; purée until smooth. Set aside.

3. In a bowl, whip cream until it starts to thicken; gradually add icing sugar, beating until soft peaks form.

4. Assembly: Put 4 pastry circles on 4 individual dessert plates. Spread with some whipped cream; top with all of remaining sliced strawberries. Top each with another pastry circle. Spread with remaining whipped cream; top with all of remaining raspberries. Add top pastry circles. Dust with additional, sifted icing sugar and serve with berry purée.

Le Cirque — New York

FIVE FRUIT AND BERRY COMPOTE

SERVES 4 TO 6

TIP

Use any combination of your favorite fruits.

TEA INFUSION:

1/2 cup	water	125 mL
2	tea bags, preferably English Breakfast tea	2
3	sprigs fresh mint	3

SYRUP:

1 1/2 cups	dry white wine	375 mL
1 1/2 cups	water	375 mL
2/3 cup	granulated sugar	150 mL
1/2 cup	Port wine	125 mL
1 tsp	vanilla extract	5 mL

FRUITS:

1	ripe mango, peeled and diced	1
2 cups	cherries, pitted	500 mL
1 cup	blueberries	250 mL
1 cup	raspberries	250 mL
12	strawberries	12

1. Make the tea infusion: In a small saucepan, bring water to a boil. Add tea bags and mint, remove from heat, cover and let stand 10 minutes. Remove tea bags from tea infusion, gently pressing to extract liquid; discard tea bags.

2. Make the syrup: In a large saucepan combine wine, water, sugar, Port, vanilla and tea infusion. Bring mixture to a boil; add fruits and return to the boil. Remove from heat.

3. Chill in refrigerator until cold. Serve in soup bowls.

Gotham Bar & Grill
— New York

RASPBERRY BOMBE

SERVES 8 TO 10

TIP

If raspberry-gelatin mixture sets before you fold in whipped cream, gently heat it over hot (not boiling) water, stirring until softened.

Preheat oven to 350° F (180° C)

10- to 12-inch (3 to 4 L) springform pan, bottom lined with buttered and floured parchment paper

8-cup (2 L) bowl

SPONGE:

6	eggs, separated	6
3/4 cup	granulated sugar	125 mL
2 tsp	vanilla extract	10 mL
1/3 cup	all-purpose flour	75 mL

DESSERT SYRUP:

1/4 cup	granulated sugar	50 mL
1/4 cup	water	50 mL
	Liqueur, any type, to taste (optional)	

RASPBERRY MOUSSE:

3/4 cup	raspberry purée	175 mL
6 tbsp	icing sugar	90 mL
1 tbsp	gelatin	15 mL
1 1/2 cups	whipping (35%) cream	375 mL

GANACHE:

6 oz	semi-sweet chocolate, chopped	175 g
1/3 cup	whipping (35%) cream	75 mL
2 tbsp	fruit jelly	25 mL
	Chopped pistachio nuts (optional)	

1. Make the sponge: In a bowl, beat egg yolks with 1/2 cup (125 mL) of the sugar until pale yellow and thick. Beat in vanilla. Gently fold in flour. In another bowl, beat egg whites until soft peaks form; gradually add remaining sugar, beating until stiff peaks form. Stir one-quarter of egg whites into yolk mixture; gently fold in remaining whites. Pour into prepared pan. Bake 20 to 25 minutes or until cake tester inserted in center comes out clean. Cool in pan on wire rack.

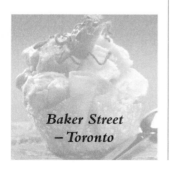

Baker Street – Toronto

2. Make the dessert syrup: In a small saucepan, combine sugar and water. Bring to a boil; remove from heat and cool. Stir in liqueur to taste, if desired.

3. Make the raspberry mousse: Stir together raspberry purée and icing sugar. Dissolve gelatin in water according to package directions; stir into raspberry mixture. Chill until mixture is slightly thickened but not set, stirring often. In another bowl, whip cream until soft peaks form. Stir one-quarter of whipped cream into raspberry mixture; gently fold in remaining whipped cream.

4. Make the ganache: In a bowl, melt the chocolate over hot (not boiling) water, stirring until smooth; cool slightly. Slowly whisk in cream. Set aside.

5. Assembly: Remove springform ring. Cut sponge horizontally into two layers. Gently lift one cake layer and place in bowl. Brush with some dessert syrup. Pour mousse on top. Trim other cake layer to fit bowl; place on top of mousse. Brush with remaining dessert syrup. Chill 2 to 4 hours.

6. Dip bowl into hot water for 5 seconds; run knife around inside edge and invert onto serving platter. Melt jelly and brush over bombe. Pour ganache over top. If ganache hardens before use, reheat slightly until it is of spreading consistency; if ganache is not stiff enough to glaze, chill for a short time. Sprinkle with chopped pistachio nuts if desired.

POACHED PEARS WITH RICOTTA PUFFS AND CRANBERRY SAUCE

SERVES 4

PEARS:

1 cup	white wine	250 mL
1 cup	water	250 mL
1 tbsp	granulated sugar	15 mL
2	large pears	2

RICOTTA PUFFS:

1 cup	ricotta cheese	250 mL
2 tbsp	semolina *or* durum wheat flour	25 mL
4 tsp	granulated sugar	20 mL
1 tbsp	soft butter	15 mL
Half	beaten egg	Half
Pinch	salt	Pinch
3 tbsp	fine bread crumbs	45 mL
1 tbsp	melted butter	15 mL
1 tbsp	granulated sugar	15 mL
1/4 tsp	cinnamon	1 mL

CRANBERRY SAUCE:

1/2 cup	cranberries	125 mL
1/2 cup	granulated sugar	125 mL
1/2 cup	red wine	125 mL
1/2 cup	water	125 mL

1. Poach the pears: In a saucepan bring wine, water and sugar to a boil; reduce heat to a simmer. Peel, core and slice pears; add to saucepan. Cook just until pears are tender. Remove from heat. Chill pears in the syrup.

2. Make the ricotta puffs: In a bowl, blend ricotta with semolina flour. In a separate bowl, beat sugar, butter, egg and salt until creamy; stir into ricotta mixture. Let rest, covered, 20 to 30 minutes. Roll into 8 small balls, adding extra flour if too sticky. Cook in saucepan of simmering water 10 minutes; turn off heat and let puffs rest in water 10 minutes longer. Meanwhile, in a small bowl stir together bread crumbs, butter, sugar

Four Seasons Yorkville
– Toronto

and cinnamon. With a slotted spoon remove puffs; cool slightly. Roll in bread crumb mixture.

3. Make the cranberry sauce: In a small saucepan combine cranberries, sugar, red wine and water; bring to a boil, reduce heat and simmer until purée consistency. Add extra sugar to taste.

4. To serve, divide puffs, pears and cranberry sauce among 4 individual dessert plates.

APPLE TORTE WITH ALMOND CREAM

SERVES 8

TIP

Chill the unbaked crust for 30 minutes after it's been patted into the pan, if you have the time.

Preheat oven to 400° F (200° C)

Baking sheet

9-inch (23 cm) flan pan with removable bottom, buttered

APPLE FILLING:

4	large Granny Smith apples	4
2/3 cup	granulated sugar	150 mL
1/4 cup	butter	50 mL
1/4 cup	Calvados *or* Amaretto	50 mL

PASTRY:

4 oz	butter	125 g
1/3 cup	granulated sugar	75 mL
2	egg yolks	2
1 1/4 cups	all–purpose flour (approximate)	300 mL

ALMOND CREAM:

1/4 cup	butter	50 mL
1/4 cup	granulated sugar	50 mL
1	egg	1
1 tbsp	grated lemon zest	15 mL
1/4 cup	ground almonds	50 mL
	cinnamon	
	granulated sugar	

1. Make the apple filling: Peel and core apples; slice thinly. Reserve one sliced apple for later. In a saucepan, combine remaining sliced apples, sugar and butter; bring to a boil, reduce heat and simmer 3 to 5 minutes. Remove from heat; stir in Calvados. Pour mixture onto baking sheet to cool.

Recipe continues...

L'Hotel – Toronto

APPLE TORTE WITH ALMOND CREAM (THIS PAGE) ➤

OVERLEAF: AMARETTO CREAM CHEESECAKE (PAGE 141) ➤

2. Make the pastry: In a bowl, cream butter with sugar until fluffy. Add egg yolks, one at a time, beating well after each. Stir in flour to form a soft dough, adding more flour if too sticky. Using hands, press into bottom and sides of flan pan. Bake 10 minutes or until golden. Cool in pan on wire rack.

3. Make the almond cream: In a bowl, cream butter with sugar until fluffy. Beat in egg and lemon rind. Fold in almonds.

4. Assembly: Strain cooked apples, reserving liquid; pour apples into crust. Pour almond cream on top. Decorate with uncooked apples; brush with some of reserved cooking liquid. Sprinkle with cinnamon and sugar to taste. Cover with foil. Bake 25 minutes; remove foil and bake 10 minutes longer. Cool on wire rack.

◄ ALMOND PEAR CREAM TART (PAGE 120)

APRICOT SUZETTES WITH CINNAMON VANILLA SAUCE

SERVES 4 TO 5

TIP

Wonton sheets are available in the specialty area of some supermarkets.

APRICOT SUZETTES:

1/2 cup	dried apricots	125 mL
1 tbsp	apricot brandy	15 mL
1 tsp	granulated sugar	5 mL
1	package wonton sheets	1
	Fresh mint leaves	

CINNAMON VANILLA SAUCE:

3/4 cup	milk	175 mL
1/2 tsp	vanilla extract	2 mL
2	egg yolks	2
1 tbsp	granulated sugar	15 mL
1/4 tsp	cinnamon	1 mL
1/4 cup	plain yogurt	50 mL

1. Make the apricot suzettes: In a saucepan, add hot water to cover to apricots; soak 1 hour. Stir in apricot brandy and sugar; bring to a boil, reduce heat and simmer 15 to 20 minutes or until apricots are tender. Drain and finely chop apricots.

2. Put one wonton sheet on a floured surface; brush with water. Top with a mint leaf; cover with another wonton sheet. Roll until thin and translucent. Brush with water; top with 1 tsp (5 mL) of diced apricots. Roll another wonton sheet until thin and place on top of apricots, pressing to seal. Repeat until diced apricots are all used. With a sharp knife, cut each into leaf shape. Cook in saucepan of simmering water 2 to 3 minutes. With a slotted spoon remove from water; cool.

3. Make the cinnamon vanilla sauce: In a small saucepan bring milk and vanilla to a boil; reduce heat and simmer 5 minutes. In a bowl, whisk together egg yolks, sugar and cinnamon. Whisk in hot milk mixture. Set bowl over hot (not boiling) water; cook, whisking, until thickened. Let cool in refrigerator. Stir in yogurt.

4. Serve suzettes with cinnamon vanilla sauce.

Four Seasons Yorkville
– Toronto

CREAM CUPS ON A STRAWBERRY PURÉE

SERVES 6 TO 8

TIP

If you don't have perforated molds, punch holes for drainage in bottom of aluminum muffin or custard cups. You can use sterile gauze pads from your medicine cabinet if you don't have cheesecloth.

This is an ideal make-ahead dessert — the molds can drain for up to 24 hours before serving.

When made using heart-shaped molds, this classic dessert is called *Coeur a la Crème*.

For a lower-fat dessert, substitute extra-smooth ricotta cheese for the cream cheese.

6 to 8 individual perforated molds lined with cheesecloth
Rimmed baking sheet

1 lb	cream cheese	500 g
3 tbsp	granulated sugar	45 mL
1 cup	whipping (35%) cream	250 mL
3	egg whites	3

STRAWBERRY PURÉE:

2 cups	fresh or frozen strawberries	500 mL
3 tbsp	icing sugar	45 mL
1 tbsp	freshly squeezed lemon juice	15 mL

1. Beat cream cheese with sugar until smooth. In a separate bowl, whip cream until stiff peaks form. In another bowl, beat egg whites until stiff peaks form; fold egg whites and whipped cream into cream cheese mixture. Pour into molds, fold cheesecloth over top and place on baking sheet. Chill 6 hours.

2. Make the strawberry purée: In a food processor, blend strawberries, icing sugar and lemon juice until smooth.

3. To serve, unfold cheesecloth and carefully invert each mold onto an individual dessert plate. Remove mold and cheesecloth. Serve with strawberry purée.

Fenton's – Toronto

Frozen Desserts

CHOCOLATE LOVERS' CHOCOLATE SUNDAE

SERVES 5

TIP

Use your favorite varieties of chocolate ice cream.

Decorate with chocolate sprinkles or a chocolate kiss.

HOT FUDGE TOPPING:

1/4 cup	butter	50 mL
4 oz	semi–sweet chocolate, chopped	125 g
1/4 cup	icing sugar	50 mL
1/2 cup	whipping (35%) cream	125 mL
1 tsp	vanilla extract	5 mL

CHOCOLATE WHIPPED CREAM:

1 cup	whipping (35%) cream	250 mL
1 tbsp	chocolate syrup	15 mL

ICE CREAM:

5	scoops chocolate chip ice cream	5
5	scoops chocolate nut fudge ice cream	5
5	scoops rocky road ice cream	5

1. Make the hot fudge topping: In a bowl over hot (not boiling) water, melt chocolate with butter, stirring until smooth. Gradually stir in icing sugar. Stir in cream; continue to stir until smooth and hot. Stir in vanilla.

2. Make the chocolate whipped cream: In a bowl, whip cream with chocolate syrup until stiff peaks form.

3. Put one scoop of each type of ice cream into each of 5 serving dishes. Divide hot fudge sauce and chocolate whipped cream among dishes. Serve immediately.

*Peppermint Park –
New York*

ICED LEMON SOUFFLÉ

TIP

For individual desserts, use six 1-cup (250 mL) dessert dishes.

This recipe may be cut in half.

For a special treat, serve this with Strawberry Coulis (see recipe for MANGO MOUSSE ON STRAWBERRY COULIS, page 37).

6-cup (1.5 L) mold

1 tsp	gelatin	5 mL
1/2 cup	freshly squeezed lemon juice	125 mL
1 cup	egg whites (about 7 eggs)	250 mL
1 cup	granulated sugar	250 mL
1 cup	whipping (35%) cream	250 mL

1. Dissolve gelatin in water according to package directions; stir in lemon juice. Set aside.

2. In a large bowl, beat egg whites until soft peaks form; gradually add sugar, beating until stiff peaks form. Set aside.

3. In a bowl, whip cream until stiff peaks form. Stir one-quarter of egg whites into lemon mixture; gently fold in remaining whites and whipped cream. Pour into mold.

4. Freeze until firm. To serve, dip mold into hot water for 5 seconds; run knife around inside edge. Invert onto serving platter.

Tavern on the Green – New York

Baked Alaska with Fruit Sauce

SERVES 8 TO 10

TIP

If you prefer, make your own sponge cake (see recipe, page 62)

8-inch (2 L) springform pan
Baking sheet

12 oz	store-bought sponge cake	375 g
2 cups	chocolate ice cream, softened	500 mL
2 cups	raspberry or strawberry sorbet, softened	500 mL
2 cups	vanilla ice cream, softened	500 mL

FRUIT SAUCE:

1/3 cup	granulated sugar	75 mL
1/4 cup	water	50 mL
1 tsp	vanilla extract	5 mL
1 cup	sliced strawberries	250 mL
1/2 cup	raspberries	125 mL
1/3 cup	blueberries	75 mL

MERINGUE:

4	egg whites	4
1/4 cup	granulated sugar	50 mL

1. Cut sponge cake into 1/4-inch (5 mm) thick slices. Line bottom and sides of springform pan with sponge cake. Press chocolate ice cream into pan, then raspberry sorbet, and finally vanilla ice cream. Top with sponge cake. Freeze 1 1/2 hours.

2. Meanwhile, make the fruit sauce: In a small saucepan combine sugar, water and vanilla; bring to a boil. Reduce heat; cook 3 to 5 minutes or until syrupy. Remove from heat. Stir in strawberries, raspberries and blueberries. Chill.

3. Before serving, make meringue: Preheat oven to 450° F (220° C). In a bowl, beat egg whites until soft peaks form; gradually add sugar, beating until stiff peaks form. Put springform pan on baking sheet. Remove springform ring; spread meringue over top and sides of frozen cake. Bake 5 to 10 minutes or until golden. Serve immediately, with fruit sauce.

Rainbow Room –
New York

ANISE ICE CREAM WITH COFFEE SAUCE

SERVES 6 TO 8

ANISE ICE CREAM:

6	egg yolks	6
3/4 cup	granulated sugar	175 mL
2 cups	milk	500 mL
1 cup	whipping (35%) cream	250 mL
2 tbsp	anisette *or* other licorice-flavored liqueur	25 mL
1 1/2 tsp	vanilla extract	7 mL

COFFEE SAUCE:

2	egg yolks	2
1 tbsp	granulated sugar	15 mL
3/4 cup	milk	175 mL
1 tbsp	instant coffee granules	15 mL
1/2 tsp	vanilla extract	2 mL

1. Make the anise ice cream: In a large bowl, whisk egg yolks with sugar. In a saucepan combine milk and cream. Heat until almost boiling; remove from heat. Whisk a little of hot milk mixture into yolk mixture, then pour back into saucepan. Whisk constantly over low heat until mixture is thick enough to coat a spoon; do not boil. Remove from heat; stir in liqueur and vanilla. Let cool in refrigerator. Freeze in ice cream maker according to manufacturer's directions.

2. Make the coffee sauce: In a bowl, whisk egg yolks with sugar. In a saucepan combine milk, instant coffee and vanilla; bring to a boil, reduce heat and simmer 5 minutes. Whisk hot milk into yolk mixture. Set bowl over hot (not boiling) water; cook, whisking, until thickened. Let cool in refrigerator.

3. Serve ice cream with coffee sauce.

*Le Bernardin —
New York*

KAHLUA FREEZE

TIP

Save the leftover egg whites — you can refrigerate them for up to 1 week or freeze them for up to 3 months. Use them later in APRICOT SOUFFLÉ (see recipe, page 43), COINTREAU CHOCOLATE CREAM WITH MERINGUE (see recipe, page 28), LEMON AND LIME MERINGUE PIE (see recipe, page 119), ALMOND LEMON MERINGUE TART (see recipe, page 132) or ALMOND DACQUOISE (see recipe, page 150).

Preheat oven to 400° F (200° C)

8-inch (2 L) springform pan, buttered and sprinkled with dry bread crumbs

SPONGE:

5	eggs	5
2/3 cup	granulated sugar	150 mL
1/3 cup	cocoa	75 mL
1/3 cup	all-purpose flour	75 mL

KAHLUA PARFAIT:

6	egg yolks	6
3/4 cup	granulated sugar	175 mL
1/4 cup	Kahlua	50 mL
2 cups	whipping (35%) cream	500 mL

VANILLA SAUCE (OPTIONAL):

2 cups	milk	500 mL
5	egg yolks	5
1/4 cup	granulated sugar	50 mL
1 tsp	vanilla extract	5 mL

CHOCOLATE SAUCE (OPTIONAL):

4 oz	semi-sweet chocolate, chopped	125 g
2 tbsp	Kahlua	25 mL

1. Make the sponge: In a bowl, beat eggs with sugar until mixture falls in ribbons when beater are lifted from the bowl. Gently fold in cocoa and flour. Pour into prepared pan. Bake 20 to 25 minutes or until cake tester inserted in center comes out clean. Cool in pan on wire rack. Remove spring-form ring. Cut cake horizontally into two layers; remove top layer. Leave bottom layer in pan and replace ring.

*Windsor Arms Hotel
— Toronto*

2. Make the Kahlua parfait: In a bowl, whisk yolks with sugar until pale yellow and thickened; beat in Kahlua. In a separate bowl, whip cream until stiff peaks form. Stir one-quarter of whipped cream into yolk mixture; gently fold in remaining whipped cream. Pour into springform pan; top with cake layer. Freeze 3 to 4 hours or until firm.

3. Make the sauces, if desired:

   Vanilla sauce. In a bowl, beat yolks with sugar until pale yellow and thick. In a saucepan, heat milk until almost boiling; remove from heat. Whisk a little of hot milk into yolk mixture, then pour back into saucepan. Whisk constantly over low heat until mixture is thick enough to coat a spoon; do not boil. Remove from heat; whisk in vanilla. Divide in half. Cool half in refrigerator.

   Chocolate sauce. In a bowl, combine half of hot vanilla sauce, chocolate and Kahlua, stirring until smooth. Cool in refrigerator.

4. Serve slices of Kahlua Freeze with sauces on the side.

HAZELNUT PARFAIT WITH CHOCOLATE SAUCE

SERVES 8

9- by 5-inch (2 L) loaf pan

HAZELNUT PARFAIT:

5	egg yolks	5
2	eggs	2
3/4 cup	granulated sugar	175 mL
1/2 cup	finely ground toasted hazelnuts	125 mL
4 oz	milk chocolate, chopped	125 g
2 1/2 cups	whipping (35%) cream	625 mL

CHOCOLATE SAUCE:

2 1/2 oz	semi-sweet chocolate	75 g
3/4 cup	whipping (35%) cream	175 mL
1 1/2 tbsp	nut liqueur (optional)	22 mL

1. Make the hazelnut parfait: In a bowl, beat egg yolks, eggs and sugar until pale yellow and thickened. Divide in half. Fold hazelnuts into one half; pour into loaf pan and set aside. In a bowl over hot (not boiling) water melt the chocolate, stirring until smooth; cool. In a separate bowl, whip cream until stiff peaks form. Stir one-quarter of whipped cream into cooled chocolate; gently fold in remaining whipped cream. Fold chocolate mixture into remaining plain egg mixture. Pour into loaf pan. Freeze 2 to 3 hours until firm.

2. Make the chocolate sauce: In a bowl over hot (not boiling) water melt chocolate, stirring until smooth; gradually whisk in cream and liqueur, if desired. Cool.

3. Dip loaf pan into hot water for 5 seconds; run knife around inside edge to loosen and invert onto serving platter. Freeze to firm up. Serve slices of parfait with chocolate sauce on the side.

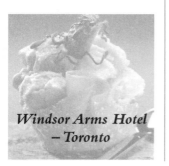

Windsor Arms Hotel – Toronto

OREO COOKIES AND CREAM ICE CREAM

TIP

To speed up cooling process at the end o step 1, place bowl in a larger bowl of cold water and ice.

If finished ice cream is too hard to scoop straight from the freezer, let stand in refrigerator 20 minutes or until slightly softened.

4	egg yolks	4
1 cup	half-and-half (10%) cream	250 mL
1/2 cup	granulated sugar	125 mL
1 tsp	vanilla extract	5 mL
1 3/4 cups	whipping (35%) cream	425 mL
1 1/3 cups	coarsely broken Oreo cookies	325 mL

1. In a bowl beat egg yolks, half-and-half (10%) cream, sugar and vanilla until well-mixed. Set bowl over hot (not boiling) water; cook, beating constantly, 5 to 7 minutes or until doubled in volume. Remove from heat. Let cool in refrigerator.

2. Stir in whipping (35%) cream. Freeze in an ice cream maker according to manufacturer's directions; when half-frozen, add Oreo cookies, and continue to freeze.

W.D. Kones - Toronto

CHOCOLATE RASPBERRY ICE CREAM

SERVES 6

TIP

To speed up cooling process at the end of step 2, place bowl in a larger bowl of cold water and ice.

If finished ice cream is too hard to scoop straight from the freezer, let stand in refrigerator 20 minutes or until slightly softened.

1 cup	fresh or frozen raspberries	250 mL
1/2 cup	granulated sugar	125 mL
5 oz	semi-sweet chocolate, chopped	150 g
4	egg yolks	4
1 cup	half-and-half (10%) cream	250 mL
1/3 cup	granulated sugar	75 mL
1 1/2 cups	whipping (35%) cream	375 mL

1. In a bowl set over boiling water, combine raspberries and sugar; cook, stirring occasionally, 10 minutes or until fruit is soft. Purée in blender or food processor. Chill.

2. In a bowl, melt chocolate over hot (not boiling) water, stirring until smooth; set aside. In another bowl set over hot (not boiling) water, beat egg yolks, half-and-half (10%) cream and sugar 5 to 7 minutes or until doubled in volume; beat in chocolate. Let cool in refrigerator.

3. Stir in whipping (35%) cream. Freeze in an ice cream maker according to manufacturer's directions; when half frozen, add raspberry purée and continue to freeze.

W.D. Kones - Toronto

MANGO SUNDAE

SERVES 6 TO 8

TIP

To speed up cooling process at end of step 2, place bowl in a larger bowl of cold water and ice.

If finished ice cream is too hard to scoop straight from the freezer, let stand in refrigerator 20 minutes or until slightly softened.

2	large ripe mangoes, peeled and chopped	2
1/3 cup	granulated sugar	75 mL
4	egg yolks	4
1 cup	half-and-half (10%) cream	250 mL
1/2 cup	granulated sugar	125 mL
1 tsp	vanilla extract	5 mL
1 3/4 cups	whipping (35%) cream	425 mL
1	ripe mango, peeled and sliced	1
1/2 cup	peach liqueur *or* peach schnapps	125 mL
	Fancy wafers	

1. In a bowl set over boiling water, combine mangoes and sugar; cook, stirring occasionally, 10 minutes or until fruit is soft. Purée in blender or food processor. Chill.

2. In a bowl set over hot (not boiling) water, beat egg yolks, half-and-half (10%) cream, sugar and vanilla 5 to 7 minutes or until doubled in volume. Let cool in refrigerator.

3. Stir in whipping (35%) cream. Freeze in an ice cream maker according to manufacturer's directions; when half frozen, add mango purée and continue to freeze.

4. Assembly: Put one scoop of mango ice cream in each individual dessert dish. Top with a thin slice of ripe mango and 1 tbsp (15 mL) peach liqueur. Serve with fancy wafers.

W.D. Kones – Toronto

PEACH FREEZE

SERVES 4

2-cup (500 mL) mold

TIP

To make peach purée, use peeled fresh ripe peaches or use drained canned peaches.

For individual parfaits, use four 1/2-cup (125 mL) molds.

This recipe doubles easily — use a 4-cup (1 L) mold or eight 1/2-cup (125 mL) molds.

You can refrigerate the left-over egg whites for up to 1 week or freeze them for up to 3 months; use them later in APRICOT SOUFFLÉ (see recipe, page 43), COINTREAU CHOCOLATE CREAM WITH MERINGUE (see recipe, page 28), LEMON AND LIME MERINGUE PIE (see recipe, page 119), ALMOND LEMON MERINGUE TART (see recipe, page 132) or ALMOND DACQUOISE (see recipe, page 150).

PARFAIT:

10	egg yolks	10
3/4 cup	granulated sugar	175 mL
1/3 cup	peach schnapps or peach liqueur	75 mL
1 tbsp	freshly squeezed lemon juice	15 mL
1 cup	35% cream	250 mL

PEACH SAUCE:

1/2 cup	peach purée	125 mL
1 tbsp	icing sugar	15 mL
1 tsp	peach schnapps *or* peach liqueur	5 mL

1. Make the parfait: In a bowl, beat egg yolks with sugar until pale yellow and thick; stir in peach schnapps and lemon juice. In a separate bowl, whip cream until stiff peaks form; fold into yolk mixture. Pour into mold. Freeze 3 hours or until set.

2. Make the peach sauce: In a bowl, stir together peach purée, icing sugar and peach schnapps.

3. Assembly: Dip mold into hot water for 5 seconds; run knife around inside edge to loosen and invert onto serving plate. Store in freezer until ready to serve. Slice and serve with peach sauce.

Windsor Arms Hotel
– Toronto

FROZEN MAPLE MOUSSE

SERVES 8

TIP

For individual mousses, use eight 1//2-cup (125 mL) molds.

4-cup (1 L) mold

3	eggs, separated	3
2 tbsp	granulated sugar	25 mL
1 1/2 tsp	brandy	7 mL
1 1/2 tsp	maple extract	7 mL
1 cup	whipping (35%) cream	250 mL
3 tbsp	icing sugar	45 mL

1. In a bowl, beat egg yolks with sugar until pale yellow and thick; beat in brandy and maple extract. In a separate bowl, whip cream until stiff; fold into yolk mixture. In another bowl, beat egg whites until soft peaks form; gradually add icing sugar, beating until stiff peaks form. Fold egg whites into yolk-cream mixture. Pour into mold. Freeze 3 hours or until set.

2. To serve, dip mold into hot water for 5 seconds; run knife around inside edge to loosen and invert onto serving plate.

King Edward Hotel – Toronto

PEPPERMINT STICK ICE CREAM

TIP

This is a great way to use up candy canes leftover from the holidays

8 oz	cream cheese	250 g
3/4 cup	granulated sugar	175 mL
1 cup	milk	250 mL
1	egg	1
2 cups	whipping (35%) cream	500 mL
1 tsp	peppermint extract, or to taste	5 mL
1/2 cup	crushed peppermint candy stick	125 mL

1. In a bowl beat cream cheese with sugar until creamy; beat in milk and egg until smooth. Stir in cream and peppermint extract. Add more peppermint extract to taste.

2. Freeze in an ice cream maker according to manufacturer's directions; when half-frozen, add crushed peppermint stick, and continue to freeze.

Peppermint Park – New York

Tarts and Flans

STRAWBERRY AND KIWI CREAM TART

TIP

You can make the pastry in a food processor if you prefer.

Substitute your favorite sliced fruits for the strawberries and kiwi fruit.

Preheat oven to 375° F (190° C)

10-inch (25 cm) flan pan with removable bottom

CRUST:

1 1/2 cups	all-purpose flour	375 mL
1/3 cup	icing sugar	75 mL
3/4 cup	butter	175 mL

PASTRY CREAM:

5	egg yolks	5
1/3 cup	granulated sugar	75 mL
1/3 cup	all-purpose flour	75 mL
1 1/2 cups	milk	375 mL
2 tbsp	butter	25 mL
1 1/2 tsp	kirsch *or* other fruit liqueur	7 mL
1 cup	sliced strawberries	250 mL
3	kiwi fruit, peeled and sliced	3
3 tbsp	fruit jelly, preferably apple	45 mL

1. Make the crust: In a bowl, stir together flour and icing sugar. With a pastry cutter or two knives, cut in butter until dough forms. Form into a ball. Pat into bottom and sides of flan pan. Bake 20 to 25 minutes or until golden. Cool in pan on wire rack.

2. Make the pastry cream: In a bowl, beat yolks with sugar until pale yellow and thick; beat in flour and set aside. In a saucepan, heat milk until almost boiling; remove from heat. Whisk a little of the hot cream into yolk mixture, then pour back into saucepan. Beat constantly over low heat 5 minutes or until thick. Remove from heat; beat in butter and kirsch. Chill.

3. Assembly: Spread cool pastry cream over crust. Decorate with sliced strawberries and kiwi fruit. In a small saucepan, melt jelly; brush over fruit.

Le Cygne – New York

APPLE TART

SERVES 6 TO 8

TIP

Try Granny Smith, Spy or Rome apples.

If you have the time, chill the unbaked crust for 30 minutes after it has been patted into the pan.

This is great with ice cream.

Preheat oven to 375° F (190° C)

8-inch (20 cm) flan pan with removable bottom

CRUST:

3/4 cup	all-purpose flour	175 mL
1/3 cup	cold butter	75 mL
1 tbsp	ice water	15 mL

TART:

4	apples	4
2 tbsp	granulated sugar	25 mL
2 tbsp	butter	25 mL
	Cinnamon	

1. Make the crust: With a pastry cutter or two knives, cut butter into flour until coarse crumb consistency is achieved. Sprinkle on water, tossing with a fork. Form into a ball. Pat into bottom and sides of pan. Bake 15 to 20 minutes or until golden. Meanwhile, prepare the filling.

2. Peel, core and thinly slice the apples; arrange slices in concentric circles on warm crust. Sprinkle with sugar; dot with butter. Bake 20 to 30 minutes or until apples are tender. Sprinkle with cinnamon to taste. Serve warm or cold.

Aurora – New York

LEMON CHIFFON TART

TIP

If you have the time, chill the unbaked crust for 30 minutes after it has been patted into the pan.

Preheat oven to 375° F (190° C)

11- to 12-inch (28 to 30 cm) flan pan with removable bottom, buttered

CRUST:

1 2/3 cups	all-purpose flour	400 mL
1 tbsp	granulated sugar	15 mL
3/4 cup	butter	175 mL
1/4 cup	ice water (approximate)	50 mL

FILLING:

6	eggs, separated	6
1/2 cup	granulated sugar	125 mL
1 cup	freshly squeezed lemon juice	250 mL
1/3 cup	butter	75 mL
3/4 cup	granulated sugar	175 mL
1 tbsp	freshly squeezed lemon juice	15 mL
	Icing sugar	

1. Make the crust: In a bowl, stir together flour and sugar. With a pastry cutter or two knives, cut in butter until coarse crumb consistency. Sprinkle on water, 1 tbsp (15 mL) at a time, tossing with a fork, until dough forms. Form into a ball. Pat into bottom and sides of flan pan. Bake 20 to 25 minutes or until golden. Cool on wire rack.

2. Make the filling: In a bowl beat egg yolks with 1/2 cup (125 mL) sugar until pale yellow and thick. Beat in 1 cup (250 mL) lemon juice and butter. Transfer to a saucepan; cook on low heat 5 to 10 minutes, stirring constantly, or until mixture thickens. Pour into a bowl; chill.

3. In a bowl, beat egg whites until soft peaks form; gradually add sugar and lemon juice, beating until stiff peaks form. Stir one-quarter of egg whites into cold lemon mixture; gently fold in remaining whites. Pour into crust. Bake 15 minutes or until golden and puffed. Cool on wire rack. Store at room temperature.

4. Serve dusted with sifted icing sugar.

La Tulipe – New York

LEMON AND LIME MERINGUE PIE

SERVES 8

TIP

You can make the pastry in a food processor if you prefer.

Use a pastry bag to pipe meringue onto hot filling for a fancier look.

Don't refrigerate meringue pies — if you do, the meringue will weep.

Fraser Morris Fine Foods — New York

Preheat oven to 375° F (190° C)

9- to 10-inch (23 to 25 cm) flan pan with removable bottom

CRUST:

1 1/2 cups	all–purpose flour	375 mL
1/3 cup	icing sugar	75 mL
3/4 cup	butter	175 mL

FILLING:

1 cup	granulated sugar	250 mL
1 cup	water	250 mL
3/4 cup	freshly squeezed lemon juice	175 mL
1/3 cup	cornstarch	75 mL
1/4 cup	freshly squeezed lime juice	50 mL
1/4 tsp	salt	1 mL
4	eggs, separated	4
1 tbsp	butter	15 mL
1/4 cup	granulated sugar	50 mL

1. Make the crust: In a bowl stir together flour and icing sugar. With a pastry cutter or two knives, cut in butter until dough forms. Form onto a ball. Pat into bottom and sides of flan pan. Bake 20 to 25 minutes or until golden. Cool in pan on wire rack. Increase oven temperature to 400° F (200° C).

2. Make the filling: In a saucepan, whisk together 1 cup (250 mL) sugar, water, lemon juice, cornstarch, lime juice and salt; cook over medium heat, stirring constantly, until thickened. Remove from heat. In a small bowl, beat egg yolks; beat into hot filling. Cook over medium heat, stirring constantly, until mixture thickens further. Remove from heat; beat in butter. Pour into crust.

3. In a bowl beat egg whites until soft peaks form; gradually add 1/4 cup (50 mL) sugar, beating until stiff peaks form. Spoon meringue over hot filling, spreading to crust; with the back of a spoon, create decorative peaks and valleys. Bake 5 minutes or until meringue is golden. Cool on wire rack.

ALMOND PEAR CREAM TART

TIP

You can make the pastry in a food processor if you prefer.

Preheat oven to 375° F (190° C)

10- to 11-inch (25 to 28 cm) flan pan with removable bottom

POACHED PEARS:

4 cups	water	1 L
2 cups	granulated sugar	500 mL
1 tbsp	grated lemon rind	15 mL
2 tbsp	lemon juice	25 mL
1 tsp	milk	5 mL
6	pears, peeled, cored and halved	6

PASTRY:

1 1/2 cups	all-purpose flour	375 mL
1/3 cup	icing sugar	75 mL
3/4 cup	butter	175 mL

ALMOND CREAM:

4 oz	almond paste	125 g
1/2 cup	granulated sugar	125 mL
1/2 cup	butter, softened	125 mL
2	eggs	2
1/2 tsp	vanilla extract	2 mL
1/3 cup	all-purpose flour	75 mL

TOPPING:

1/2 cup	apple jelly	125 mL
2 tbsp	fruit liqueur, preferably pear	25 mL
1/4 cup	chopped nuts (optional)	50 mL

1. Poach the pears: In a saucepan bring water, sugar, lemon rind, lemon juice and milk to a boil; add pears, reduce heat to a simmer and cook 10 to 15 minutes or until pears are tender. Remove from heat; set aside.

2. Make the pastry: In a bowl stir together flour and icing sugar. With a pastry cutter or two knives, cut in butter until dough forms. Form into a ball. Pat into bottom and sides of flan pan. Bake 20 minutes or until golden. Cool in pan on wire rack.

John Clancy's –
New York

3. Make the almond cream: In a bowl, beat almond paste with sugar until smooth; beat in butter. Beat in eggs and vanilla until smooth. Stir in flour until combined. Chill until use.

4. Assembly: Spread almond cream over cooled crust. Drain pears, discarding syrup; slice thinly and arrange on top of almond cream. Bake 45 minutes or until almond cream is set. Cool on wire rack.

5. Make topping: In a small saucepan melt jelly; stir in liqueur. Brush over tart. Sprinkle with nuts, if desired.

CHOCOLATE PECAN PIE

SERVES 8

TIP

You can make the pastry in a food processor if you prefer.

Preheat oven to 350° F (180° C)

9- to 10-inch (23 to 25 cm) flan pan with removable bottom, buttered

CRUST:

1 1/2 cups	all–purpose flour	375 mL
1/3 cup	icing sugar	75 mL
3/4 cup	butter	175 mL

FILLING:

3 oz	semi–sweet chocolate	90 g
2 tbsp	butter	25 mL
1 cup	corn syrup	250 mL
1 cup	granulated sugar	250 mL
3	eggs	3
1 cup	pecan halves	250 mL
1/4 cup	miniature chocolate chips (optional)	50 mL

1. Make the crust: In a bowl, stir together flour and icing sugar. With a pastry cutter or two knives, cut in butter until dough forms. Form into a ball. Pat into bottom and sides of flan pan. Bake 15 to 20 minutes or until golden. Cool in pan on wire rack.

2. Make the filling: In a bowl, melt the chocolate with butter over hot (not boiling) water, stirring until smooth; set aside. In a saucepan, heat corn syrup with sugar until liquid; remove from heat and beat into chocolate mixture. Stir in pecans and, if desired, chocolate chips. Pour into crust. Bake about 45 minutes or until slightly loose just at center. Cool on wire rack.

Gindi – New York

WALNUT LEMON BUTTER TART

SERVES 8 TO 10

Preheat oven to 350° F (180° C)

11-inch (28 cm) flan pan with removable bottom

PASTRY:

1 1/2 cup	cake and pastry flour	375 mL
1 cup	walnut pieces	250 mL
1/2 cup	butter, softened	125 mL
1/4 cup	granulated sugar	50 mL
1	small egg	1
1	small egg yolk	1

FILLING:

1 1/4 cups	melted butter	300 mL
1 1/4 cups	granulated sugar	300 mL
4	large eggs	4
4	large egg yolks	4
2 tbsp	grated lemon rind	25 mL
1/2 cup	freshly squeezed lemon juice	125 mL
2 tsp	vanilla extract	10 mL
	Icing sugar	
	Finely chopped walnuts	

1. Make the pastry: Sift cake and pastry flour. In a food processor, combine walnuts with 1/2 cup (125 mL) of the flour until finely ground. In a bowl, cream butter with sugar until fluffy; beat in walnut mixture and remaining flour. Stir in egg and egg yolk until dough forms; form into a ball. Pat into bottom and sides of flan pan; chill 30 minutes. Bake 20 to 30 minutes or until golden. Cool on wire rack.

2. Make the filling: In a saucepan whisk together butter, sugar, eggs, egg yolks, lemon rind, lemon juice and vanilla. Cook over medium–low heat, stirring constantly, 5 minutes or until thickened; do not boil. Reduce heat to low; beat 2 minutes longer. Pour into crust. Chill.

3. Serve dusted with sifted icing sugar and sprinkled with finely chopped walnuts.

Between the Bread –
New York

APPLE CREAM PIE

SERVES 8

TIP

If you have the time, chill the unbaked crust for 30 minutes after it has been patted into the pan.

For a two-crust pie, double the pastry. Pat half into pan, top with apples, then custard. Roll other half of pastry into a circle, place over unbaked apples and custard and crimp edges. Bake until golden, about 30 minutes.

Preheat oven to 375° F (190° C)

9 to 10-inch (23 to 25 cm) flan pan with removable bottom

CRUST:

1 1/4 cups	all–purpose flour	300 mL
1 tsp	granulated sugar	5 mL
1/3 cup	cold butter	75 mL
2 tbsp	lard	25 mL
3 tbsp	ice water	45 mL

FILLING:

4	apples	4
1/2 cup	granulated sugar	125 mL
1/2 cup	cream	125 mL
1	egg	1
1 tsp	kirsch	5 mL
	Cinnamon	

1. Make the crust: In a bowl, stir together flour and sugar. With a pastry cutter or two knives, cut in butter and lard until coarse crumb consistency. Sprinkle on water, 1 tbsp (15 mL) at a time, tossing with a fork, until dough forms; form into a ball. Pat into bottom and sides of flan pan. Bake 15 to 20 minutes or until golden. Cool on wire rack.

2. Make the filling: Peel, core and thinly slice apples; arrange on crust. Bake 15 minutes. Meanwhile, in a bowl, whisk together sugar, cream, egg and kirsch. Pour over apples and continue to bake 20 minutes or until custard is set. Cool on wire rack. Sprinkle with cinnamon to taste.

Lutece - New York

ORANGE CREAM TART

SERVES 8

TIP

Make the crust in a food processor if you like.

Preheat oven to 375° F (190° C)

9- to 10-inch (23 to 25 cm) flan pan with removable bottom

CRUST:

1 1/2 cups	all-purpose flour	375 mL
1/3 cup	icing sugar	75 mL
3/4 cup	butter	175 mL

PASTRY CREAM:

5	egg yolks	5
1/3 cup	granulated sugar	75 mL
1/3 cup	all-purpose flour	75 mL
1 1/2 cups	milk	375 mL
2 tbsp	butter	25 mL
1 1/2 tsp	orange liqueur	7 mL

TOPPING:

4	large oranges	4
1/4 cup	apple jelly	50 mL

1. Make the crust: In a bowl stir together flour and icing sugar. With a pastry cutter or two knives, cut in butter until dough forms. Form into a ball. Pat into bottom and sides of flan pan. Bake 20 to 25 minutes or until golden. Cool in pan on wire rack.

2. Make the pastry cream: In a bowl, beat yolks with sugar until pale yellow and thick; beat in flour and set aside. In a saucepan, heat milk until almost boiling; remove from heat. Whisk a little of the hot cream into yolk mixture, then pour back into saucepan. Beat constantly over low heat 5 minutes or until thick. Remove from heat; beat in butter and liqueur. Pour onto cooled crust. Chill.

3. Before serving, with a sharp knife cut away peel, pith and skin of oranges. Carefully cut segments away from skin; arrange on top of tart. In a small saucepan melt jelly. Brush over tart.

Lutece – New York

RHUBARB CUSTARD TART

SERVES 6 TO 8

TIP

If you use frozen rhubarb, thaw and drain before using.

You can make the pastry in a food processor if you prefer.

Preheat oven to 375° F (190° C)

8-inch (2 L) springform pan

CRUST:

1 1/2 cups	all-purpose flour	375 mL
1/3 cup	icing sugar	75 mL
3/4 cup	butter	175 mL

FILLING:

5 cups	sliced rhubarb	1.25 L
1 cup	granulated sugar	250 mL
3 tbsp	all-purpose flour	45 mL
2	eggs	2
1/4 cup	melted butter	50 mL

TOPPING:

1 cup	chopped nuts	250 mL
1/2 cup	all-purpose flour	125 mL
1/3 cup	packed brown sugar	75 mL
1/3 cup	granulated sugar	75 mL
1 tbsp	cinnamon	15 mL
1/2 cup	butter, softened	125 mL

1. Make the crust: In a bowl, stir together flour and icing sugar. With a pastry cutter or two knives, cut in butter until dough forms. Form into a ball. Pat into bottom and sides of springform pan. Bake 15 to 20 minutes or until golden. Cool in pan on wire rack.

2. Make the filling: Put rhubarb in crust. In a bowl, stir together sugar and flour. In a separate bowl beat eggs and butter; stir into dry ingredients. Pour over rhubarb.

3. Make the topping: In a bowl, stir together nuts, flour, brown sugar, sugar and cinnamon. Cut in butter until mixture is crumbly. Sprinkle over filling. Bake 35 to 45 minutes or until rhubarb is tender. If topping browns too quickly, cover pan with foil. Cool on wire rack.

Dessert Peddler –
Toronto

HARVEST PIE

TIP

You can make the pastry in a food processor if you prefer.

Preheat oven to 375° F (190° C)

9-inch (2.5 L) springform pan

CRUST:

1 1/2 cups	all-purpose flour	375 mL
1/3 cup	icing sugar	75 mL
3/4 cup	butter	175 mL

FILLING:

2 cups	peeled, sliced apples	500 mL
1 cup	drained canned mandarin oranges	250 mL
1 cup	peeled, sliced pears	250 mL
1 cup	raisins	250 mL
3/4 cup	granulated sugar	175 mL
1/4 cup	all-purpose flour	50 mL
1 tsp	cinnamon	5 mL
1/4 tsp	nutmeg	1 mL

TOPPING:

1 cup	chopped pecans	250 mL
1/2 cup	all-purpose flour	125 mL
2/3 cup	granulated sugar	150 mL
1 tbsp	cinnamon	15 mL
1/2 cup	butter	125 mL

1. Make the crust: In a bowl, stir together flour and icing sugar. With a pastry cutter or two knives, cut in butter until dough forms. Form into a ball. Pat into bottom and sides of springform pan. Bake 15 to 20 minutes or until golden. Cool in pan on wire rack.

2. Make the filling: In a bowl, combine apples, mandarin oranges, pears, raisins, sugar, flour, cinnamon and nutmeg; toss until dry ingredients coat the fruit. Spoon into crust.

3. Make topping: In a bowl, stir together pecans, flour, sugar and cinnamon. Cut in butter until crumbly. Sprinkle over filling. Bake 45 minutes or until fruit is tender. If topping browns too quickly, cover pan with foil. Cool on wire rack.

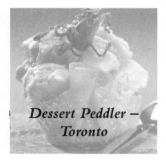

Dessert Peddler –
Toronto

Strawberry Rhubarb Linzer Pie

Serves 8 to 10

TIP

You can use frozen rhubarb — thaw and drain before using.

Preheat oven to 400° F (200° C)

10-inch (3 L) springform pan, buttered

Pastry:

1 cup	cold butter	250 mL
1 cup	granulated sugar	250 mL
2 cups	all-purpose flour	500 mL
1/4 cup	ground almonds	50 mL
1/2 tsp	cinnamon	2 mL
Pinch	ground cloves	Pinch
2	egg yolks	2

Filling:

2 tbsp	butter	25 mL
1/2 cup	granulated sugar	125 mL
6 cups	sliced rhubarb	1.5 L
1 tbsp	cornstarch	15 mL
2 cups	strawberries, hulled and halved	500 mL
1 tbsp	grated orange rind	15 mL

1. Make the pastry: Cut butter into small pieces. Put in food processor with sugar; blend until creamy. Add flour, almonds, cinnamon and cloves; blend until crumbly. Add egg yolks; blend until dough forms. Form into a ball, wrap in plastic wrap and chill 1 1/2 hours.

2. Make the filling: In a large saucepan, melt butter with 1/4 cup (50 mL) of the sugar over medium heat. Stir in rhubarb; cook, covered, 5 minutes or until rhubarb is tender when pierced with a fork.

Dufflet — Toronto

Chocolate Pecan Pie (page 122) ➤

Overleaf: Strawberry Cream Dacquoise (page 152) ➤

Strain, reserving liquid; return rhubarb to saucepanand hold warm over low heat. Stir cornstarch and remaining sugar into rhubarb juice until smooth; stir into rhubarb. Cook until mixture thickens. Remove from heat; stir in strawberries and orange rind. Cool to room temperature.

3. Assembly: Pat two-thirds of pastry onto bottom and up sides of springform pan. Pour filling into pan. Crumble remaining pastry on top of filling. Bake 15 minutes; reduce heat to 325° F (160° C) and bake 20 minutes longer or until crust is golden. Cool on wire rack.

◄ STRAWBERRY KIWI CREAM CHEESE CHOCOLATE FLAN (PAGE 136)

Sour Cream Apple Pie

Serves 8

Preheat oven to 400° F (200° C)

9-inch (2.5 L) springform pan *or*
9-inch (23 cm) pie plate,
buttered and floured

CRUST:

1 1/2 cups	graham wafer crumbs	375 mL
1/2 cup	melted butter	125 mL
1/4 cup	granulated sugar	50 mL

FILLING:

2	eggs	2
1 1/2 cups	sour cream	375 mL
1 cup	granulated sugar	250 mL
3 tbsp	all-purpose flour	45 mL
1 tsp	cinnamon	5 mL
3/4 tsp	vanilla extract	4 mL
6	apples	6

TOPPING:

1/3 cup	all-purpose flour	75 mL
1/3 cup	granulated sugar	75 mL
3/4 tsp	cinnamon	5 mL
3 tbsp	cold butter	45 mL

1. Make the crust: In a bowl, stir together graham crumbs, butter and sugar; press onto bottom and sides of prepared pan. Chill.

2. Make the filling: In a bowl, blend eggs, sour cream, sugar, flour, cinnamon and vanilla. Peel and core apples; cut into 1-inch (2.5 cm) pieces. Stir into filling. Pour into crust. Bake 15 minutes; reduce heat to 350° F (180° C) and bake 30 minutes. Meanwhile, prepare the topping.

3. Topping: In a small bowl, stir together flour, sugar and cinnamon; cut in butter to a coarse crumb consistency. After pie has baked 30 minutes, sprinkle topping over pie; increase heat to 400° F (200° C) and bake 15 minutes longer or until topping is golden. Cool on wire rack.

Just Desserts –
Toronto

TARTE TATIN

SERVES 6 TO 8

TIP

This tart is best served the day it is made.

Preheat oven to 350° F (180° C)

9- or 10-inch (23 or 25 cm) pie plate lined with foil

1/4 cup	butter, softened	50 mL
7	Granny Smith apples	7
1 1/2 tbsp	granulated sugar	22 mL
1 1/2 tsp	cinnamon	7 mL
3 tbsp	butter	45 mL
1/3 cup	granulated sugar	75 mL
8	sheets phyllo pastry	8
2 tsp	melted butter	10 mL

1. Spread 1/4 cup (50 mL) butter over bottom and sides of prepared pan. Peel and core apples; slice each into 6 pieces and arrange in pan. In a small bowl, stir together 1 1/2 tbsp (22 mL) sugar and cinnamon; sprinkle over apples. In a small saucepan, melt butter with sugar; pour over apples.

2. Fold each phyllo sheet in half. Lay on top of apples one at a time, tucking in edges after each sheet. Brush top sheet with melted butter. Bake 30 minutes or until golden. Cool on wire rack 2 hours. Place serving plate on top of pie plate and quickly invert. Blot excess liquid with paper towels.

Patachou – Toronto

ALMOND LEMON MERINGUE TART

TIP

Use a pastry bag to pipe meringue onto hot filling for a fancier look.

You'll need 11 eggs in total for this tart.

Don't refrigerate meringue pies— if you do, the meringue will weep.

Preheat oven to 375° F (190° C)

8- to 9-inch (20 to 23 cm) flan pan with removable bottom, buttered

PASTRY:

1/2 cup	butter, softened	125 mL
1/3 cup	granulated sugar	75 mL
2	egg yolks	2
1 1/4 cups	all-purpose flour (approximate)	300 mL

ALMOND CREAM:

1/4 cup	butter	50 mL
1/4 cup	granulated sugar	50 mL
1	egg	1
1 tbsp	grated lemon rind	15 mL
1/4 cup	ground almonds	50 mL

LEMON FILLING:

4	eggs	4
4	egg yolks	4
1/2 cup	granulated sugar	125 mL
6 tbsp	freshly squeezed lemon juice	90 mL
2 tbsp	butter, softened	25 mL

MERINGUE:

5	egg whites	5
1/2 cup	granulated sugar	125 mL

1. Make the pastry: In a bowl cream butter with sugar until fluffy; beat in egg yolks, one at a time. Stir in flour until dough forms; add more flour if dough is too sticky. Form into a ball, wrap in plastic wrap and chill 30 minutes.

2. Make the almond cream: In a bowl cream butter with sugar until fluffy; beat in egg and lemon rind. Fold in almonds.

3. Pat the chilled dough into bottom and sides of flan pan; spread with almond cream. Bake 30 minutes or until pastry is golden. Cool on wire rack. Increase oven to 475° F (240° C).

L'Hotel – Toronto

4. Make lemon filling: In a bowl set over hot (not boiling) water, whisk together eggs, egg yolks, sugar, lemon juice and butter; cook 15 minutes, stirring occasionally, or until thickened. Pour over almond cream.

5. Make the meringue: In a bowl, beat egg whites until soft peaks form; gradually add sugar, beating until stiff peaks form. Spoon meringue over hot filling, spreading to crust; with the back of a spoon, create decorative peaks and valleys. Bake 5 minutes or until meringue is golden. Cool on wire rack.

PLUM TART

SERVES 6 TO 8

Preheat oven to 375° F (190° C)
9 to 10-inch (23 to 25 cm) flan pan with removable bottom

PASTRY:

1/2 cup	butter, softened	125 mL
1/3 cup	granulated sugar	75 mL
1	egg	1
1 tsp	vanilla extract	5 mL
1 1/4 cups	all-purpose flour (approximate)	300 mL

FILLING:

1/2 cup	butter	125 mL
1/2 cup	granulated sugar	125 mL
2 tbsp	cognac	25 mL
2 lbs	plums, halved	1 kg

1. Make the pastry: In a bowl, cream butter with sugar until fluffy; beat in egg and vanilla. Stir in flour until dough forms; add more flour if dough is too sticky, add a little ice water if too dry. Form into a ball, wrap in plastic wrap and chill 30 minutes.

2. Make the filling: In a large saucepan, melt butter; stir in sugar and 1 tbsp (15 mL) of the cognac and bring to a boil. Stir in plums; reduce heat to medium, cover and cook 5 minutes. Stir in remaining cognac. Let cool in refrigerator.

3. Pat pastry into pan. Bake 15 to 20 minutes or until golden. Spoon filling into crust; increase oven to 450° F (230° C) and bake 5 minutes longer. Cool on wire rack. Store at room temperature.

Patachou – Toronto

MAPLE PECAN TART

SERVES 8

TIP

If you have the time, chill the unbaked crust for 30 minutes after it has been patted into the pan.

Preheat oven to 375° F (190° C)

9- to 10-inch (23 to 25 cm) flan pan with removable bottom

PASTRY:

1/2 cup	butter, softened	125 mL
1/4 cup	granulated sugar	50 mL
1/2	beaten egg	1/2
1 1/2 tsp	milk	7 mL
1/2 tsp	vanilla extract	2 mL
Pinch	salt	Pinch
1 1/2 cups	all-purpose flour	375 mL
1/3 cup	ground almonds	75 mL

FILLING:

2/3 cup	maple syrup	150 mL
1/2 cup	granulated sugar	125 mL
3	eggs	3
1 1/2 cups	chopped pecans or pecan halves	375 mL
2 tbsp	butter	25 mL

1. Make the pastry: In a bowl, cream together butter and sugar; beat in egg, milk, vanilla and salt. Fold in flour and almonds to form a dough. Form into a ball. Pat into bottom and sides of flan pan. Bake 15 to 20 minutes or until golden. Cool on wire rack. Lower heat to 325° F (160° C).

2. Make the filling: In a saucepan, heat maple syrup with sugar until sugar dissolves; remove from heat and cool slightly. Beat in eggs, pecans and butter. Pour into crust. Bake 20 to 30 minutes or until firm to the touch.

Sutton Place – Toronto

STRAWBERRY KIWI CREAM CHEESE CHOCOLATE FLAN

SERVES 8

TIP

When melting chocolate over hot water, don't let the water boil and don't let the bowl touch the water — if the water boils or comes in contact with the bowl, the chocolate will scorch.

Preheat oven to 375° F (190° C)

9- to 10-inch (23 to 25 cm) flan pan with removable bottom

PASTRY:

1 1/2 cups	all-purpose flour	375 mL
1/4 cup	granulated sugar	50 mL
3/4 cup	butter	175 mL
1 1/2 tsp	white vinegar	7 mL

FILLING:

2 oz	semi-sweet chocolate	60 g
1 tbsp	whipping (35%) cream	15 mL
8 oz	cream cheese	250 g
3 tbsp	icing sugar	45 mL
2 tbsp	milk	25 mL
1/4 tsp	vanilla extract	1 mL

TOPPING:

2 cups	strawberries, halved	500 mL
2	kiwi fruit, peeled and sliced	2
2 tbsp	red currant or apple jelly	25 mL
	Toasted sliced almonds	
	Icing sugar	

1. Make the pastry: In a bowl, stir together flour and sugar. With a pastry cutter or two knives, cut in butter to achieve a coarse crumb consistency. Sprinkle in vinegar, tossing with a fork. Form into a ball, wrap in plastic wrap and chill 30 minutes. Pat into bottom and sides of flan pan. Freeze 5 to 10 minutes. Bake 15 to 20 minutes or until golden. Cool on wire rack.

2. Make the filling: In a bowl, melt the chocolate over hot (not boiling) water, stirring until smooth. Remove from heat; stir in cream. Pour into crust; chill for a few minutes. In a bowl beat together cream cheese, icing sugar, milk and vanilla until smooth. Spread over chocolate; chill a few minutes.

Sweet Sue Pastries –
Toronto

3. Before serving, decorate with strawberries and kiwi fruit. In a small saucepan, melt jelly; brush over flan. Garnish with almonds and dust with sifted icing sugar.

Cheesecakes

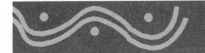

SOUR CREAM ALMOND CHEESECAKE

SERVES 8 TO 10

TIP

Toast nuts in a nonstick skillet over medium-high heat, stirring occasionally, until golden and fragrant. Or, toast in a 350° F (180° C) oven for about 10 minutes.

Preheat oven to 325° F (160° C)

8-inch (2 L) springform pan, buttered

CRUST:

1 cup	graham wafer crumbs	250 mL
1/4 cup	melted butter	50 mL
2 tbsp	chopped almonds	25 mL
2 tbsp	granulated sugar	25 mL

FILLING:

1 1/2 cups	sliced almonds, toasted	375 mL
1 1/4 lb	cream cheese	625 g
3/4 cup	granulated sugar	175 mL
2	eggs	2
1/2 cup	sour cream	125 mL
1/2 cup	whipping (35%) cream	125 mL
1 1/2 tbsp	vanilla extract	22 mL
	Toasted sliced almonds	
	Icing sugar	

1. Make the crust: In a bowl, blend graham wafer crumbs, butter, almonds and sugar. Pat onto bottom of pan. Chill.

2. Make the filling: In a food processor, chop almonds until finely ground; set aside. In a bowl, beat cream cheese with sugar until smooth; add eggs, one at a time, beating well after each. Stir in sour cream, cream and vanilla until well-mixed. Fold in ground almonds. Pour into prepared crust.

3. Bake 60 to 70 minutes or until cake tester inserted in center comes out clean. Cool to room temperature on wire rack; chill. Before serving, decorate with toasted sliced almonds and dust with icing sugar.

The Silver Palate –
New York

AMARETTO CREAM CHEESECAKE

SERVES 10 TO 12

Preheat oven to 325° F (160° C)

8-inch (2 L) springform pan

CRUST:

1 cup	graham wafer crumbs	250 mL
3 tbsp	butter, softened	45 mL
1 1/2 tsp	ground almonds	7 mL

FILLING:

1 1/2 lbs	cream cheese	750 g
1/2 cup	granulated sugar	125 mL
3	eggs	3
1/3 cup	sour cream	75 mL
2/3 cup	whipping (35%) cream	150 mL
1/2 cup	Amaretto liqueur	125 mL
	Toasted sliced almonds (optional)	
	Sliced fresh fruit (optional)	

1. Make the crust: In a bowl, blend graham wafer crumbs, butter and almonds until crumbs hold together. Pat onto bottom of pan. Chill.

2. Make the filling: In a bowl, beat cream cheese with sugar until smooth; add eggs, one at a time, beating well after each. Beat in sour cream. Stir in cream and amaretto. Pour into crust.

3. Bake 1 hour or until just slightly loose at the center. Cool to room temperature on wire rack; chill. If desired, decorate with toasted sliced almonds or sliced fresh fruit before serving.

Windows on the World – New York

CARNEGIE'S FAMOUS CHEESECAKE

SERVES 12

TIP

The sugar dough crust, instead of a traditional graham wafer crust, makes this cheesecake unusual as well as delicious.

Preheat oven to 400° F (200° C)

Butter a 9-inch (2.5 L) springform pan

PASTRY:

3/4 cup	butter, softened	175 mL
2/3 cup	granulated sugar	150 mL
1 1/2 cups	all-purpose flour	375 mL
1 tbsp	grated lemon rind	15 mL
1 tsp	vanilla extract	5 mL

FILLING:

2 lbs	cream cheese	1 kg
1 cup	granulated sugar	250 mL
2	eggs	2
2 tbsp	cornstarch	25 mL
1 tbsp	lemon juice	15 mL
1 1/2 tsp	vanilla extract	7 mL
1 cup	sour cream	250 mL
	Fresh berries (optional)	
	Icing sugar (optional)	

1. Make the pastry: In a bowl, cream butter with sugar until fluffy; stir in flour, lemon rind and vanilla to form a dough. Pat onto bottom and sides of pan. Bake 15 to 20 minutes or until golden. Cool on wire rack.

2. Make the filling: In a bowl, beat cream cheese with sugar until smooth; beat in eggs, one at a time, beating well after each. Beat in cornstarch, lemon juice and vanilla. Fold in sour cream. Pour into crust.

3. Bake 45 to 50 minutes or until just slightly loose at the center. Cool to room temperature on wire rack. Chill. If desired, serve with fresh berries and dust with icing sugar.

Carnegie Deli – New York

MISS GRIMBLE'S ABC
CHEESECAKE

SERVES 10 TO 12

Preheat oven to 350° F (190° C)

9-inch (2.5 L) springform pan

CRUST:

2 cups	graham wafer crumbs	500 mL
1/4 cup	melted butter	50 mL

FILLING:

1 1/2 lbs	cream cheese	750 g
1 cup	granulated sugar	250 mL
4	eggs, separated	4
1 tsp	vanilla extract	5 mL

TOPPING:

2 cups	sour cream	500 mL
2 tbsp	granulated sugar	25 mL
1 tsp	vanilla extract	5 mL

1. Make the crust: In a bowl, mix graham wafer crumbs with butter; pat onto bottom and up sides of pan. Chill.

2. Make the filling: In a bowl, beat cream cheese with sugar until smooth; beat in egg yolks and vanilla. In a separate bowl, beat egg whites until stiff. Stir one-quarter of whites into cream cheese mixture; gently fold in remaining whites. Pour into pan. Bake 40 to 50 minutes or until just slightly loose at center. Remove from oven; increase oven heat to 475° F (240° C).

3. Make the topping: In a bowl, stir together sour cream, sugar and vanilla. Spoon over hot cheesecake. Bake 5 minutes. Cool to room temperature on wire rack. Chill.

Miss Grimble's —
New York

APPLE CINNAMON CHEESECAKE

Preheat oven to 325° F (160° C)

9-inch (2.5 L) springform pan

CRUST:

2 cups	graham wafer crumbs	500 mL
1/2 cup	granulated sugar	125 mL
1/2 cup	melted butter	125 mL
1/2 tsp	cinnamon	2 mL

FILLING:

1 1/2 lbs	cream cheese	750 g
1 cup	granulated sugar	250 mL
4	eggs	4
1 tsp	lemon juice	5 mL
1 tsp	vanilla extract	5 mL
1 cup	peeled, diced apples	250 mL
1 tbsp	all-purpose flour	15 mL
1 tbsp	cinnamon	15 mL

TOPPING:

2 cups	sour cream	500 mL
1/4 cup	granulated sugar	50 mL
1 tsp	vanilla extract	5 mL

1. Make the crust: In a bowl, combine graham wafer crumbs, sugar, butter and cinnamon; press onto bottom and up sides of pan. Chill.

2. Make the filling: In a bowl, beat cream cheese with sugar until smooth; add eggs, one at time, beating well after each. Stir in lemon juice and vanilla. In a small bowl, stir together apples, flour and cinnamon; fold into cream cheese mixture. Pour into crust.

3. Bake 55 to 60 minutes or until just slightly loose at the center. Cool on wire rack 20 minutes. Meanwhile make the topping.

4. Topping: In a bowl, stir together sour cream, sugar and vanilla. Spoon over cheesecake. Bake 15 minutes. Cool to room temperature on wire rack. Chill.

Carole's Cheesecake Co.– Toronto

RICH CHOCOLATE CHEESECAKE

SERVES 10 TO 12

TIP

When melting chocolate over hot water, don't let the water boil and don't let the bowl touch the water — if the water boils or comes in contact with the bowl, the chocolate will scorch.

Preheat oven to 250° F (120° C)

9-inch (2.5 L) springform pan

CRUST:

2 cups	graham wafer crumbs	500 mL
3 tbsp	melted butter	45 mL
1 1/2 tbsp	cocoa	22 mL

FILLING:

6 oz	semi-sweet chocolate, chopped	175 g
1 1/2 lbs	cream cheese	750 g
1 cup	granulated sugar	250 mL
3	eggs	3
3 tbsp	all-purpose flour	45 mL
2 tbsp	cocoa	25 mL
2 tbsp	sour cream	25 mL
2 tsp	vanilla extract	10 mL
	Chocolate shavings (optional)	
	Whipped cream (optional)	

1. Make the crust: In a bowl, stir together graham wafer crumbs, butter and cocoa; press onto bottom and up sides of pan. Bake 15 minutes. Cool on wire rack. Increase oven to 350° F (180° C).

2. Make the filling: In a bowl, melt chocolate over hot (not boiling) water, stirring until smooth; set aside. In a bowl, beat cream cheese with sugar until smooth; beat in eggs, one at a time, beating well after each. Beat in flour, cocoa and vanilla until smooth. Beat in chocolate until well-mixed. Pour into crust.

3. Bake 40 to 45 minutes or until just slightly loose at center. Cool to room temperature on wire rack. Chill. If desired, serve decorated with chocolate shavings and whipped cream.

Dessert Peddler —
Toronto

ORANGE CHEESECAKE

Preheat oven to 325° F (160° C)

9- to 10-inch (2.5 to 3 L) springform pan, buttered

CRUST:

1 1/2 cups	vanilla wafer crumbs	375 mL
6 tbsp	butter, softened	90 mL
1/4 cup	granulated sugar	50 mL
1 tbsp	grated orange rind	15 mL

FILLING:

3/4 cup	granulated sugar	175 mL
1 tbsp	grated orange rind	15 mL
2 lbs	cream cheese, cut into pieces	1 kg
6	eggs	6
3/4 cup	orange juice concentrate	175 mL
	Orange segments (optional)	
	Apple jelly (optional)	

1. Make the crust: In a bowl, blend vanilla wafer crumbs, butter, sugar and orange rind; pat onto bottom and up sides of pan. Chill.

2. Make the filling: In a food processor, blend sugar with orange rind. Add cream cheese a bit at a time, mixing until smooth. Beat in eggs, one at a time, beating well after each. Mix in orange juice concentrate. Pour into crust.

3. Bake 1 hour 15 minutes or until just slightly loose at the center. Cool to room temperature on wire rack. Chill. If desired, decorate with orange segments and glaze with melted apple jelly before serving.

Inn on the Park
— Toronto

ALMOND RICOTTA CHEESECAKE

TIP

Use extra smooth ricotta for the smoothest-textured cheesecake.

Preheat oven to 375° F (190° C)

9-inch (2.5 L) springform pan

CRUST:

1 cup	butter, softened	250 mL
1 cup	granulated sugar	250 mL
2	egg yolks	2
2 cups	all-purpose flour	500 mL
1 1/4 cups	ground almonds	300 mL
1/2 tsp	cinnamon	2 mL

FILLING:

3 cups	ricotta cheese	750 mL
1/3 cup	granulated sugar	75 mL
4	eggs, separated	4
1/2 tsp	almond extract	2 mL
	Icing sugar	

1. Make the crust: In a bowl, cream butter with sugar until fluffy; beat in egg yolks. Stir in flour, almonds and cinnamon until crumbly. Reserve one-third of mixture for topping. Pat remaining two-thirds of mixture onto bottom and sides of springform pan; chill.

2. Make the filling: In a bowl, beat ricotta with sugar until smooth; beat in egg yolks and almond extract. In a separate bowl, beat egg whites until stiff peaks form. Stir one-quarter of egg whites into ricotta mixture; gently fold in remaining whites. Pour into prepared crust. Crumble reserved crust mixture over top. Bake 50 to 60 minutes or until cake tester inserted in center comes out almost dry. Turn heat off; cool cheesecake in oven with door open. Chill. Serve dusted with sifted icing sugar.

Ferrara – New York

Brûlée, Dacquoise and Other Desserts

ALMOND DACQUOISE

SERVES 6 TO 8

Preheat oven to 300° F (150° C)
3 baking sheets lined with parchment paper

MERINGUE:

1 1/4 cups	toasted ground almonds	300 mL
3/4 cup	granulated sugar	175 mL
2 cups	icing sugar	500 mL
1 tbsp	cornstarch	15 mL
10	egg whites	10
3 tbsp	granulated sugar	45 mL

BUTTER CREAM:

2/3 cup	granulated sugar	150 mL
1/2 cup	corn syrup	125 mL
4	egg yolks	4
1 2/3 cups	butter, cut in pieces and softened	400 mL
1/4 cup	Amaretto liqueur	50 mL

1. Using the base of an 8-inch (2 L) springform pan as a template, draw an 8-inch (20 cm) circle on each parchment-lined baking sheet. Butter and flour parchment paper.

2. Make the meringue: In a bowl, stir together ground almonds and 3/4 cup (175 mL) sugar. Sift icing sugar and cornstarch into almond mixture; mix and set aside. In a bowl, beat egg whites until soft peaks form; gradually add sugar, beating until stiff peaks form. Gently fold almond mixture into egg whites. Spoon most of meringue onto circles on parchment paper, or pipe onto circles using a pastry bag. Spoon or pipe remaining meringue into fingers of any size on parchment paper next to meringue circles. Bake 75 to 90 minutes or until meringue is golden and crisp. Cool on wire racks.

La Cote Basque –
New York

3. Make the butter cream: In a saucepan over medium heat, cook sugar and corn syrup, stirring, until mixture boils; remove from heat. In a bowl, beat egg yolks until pale yellow and thickened; add hot corn syrup mixture, beating 3 to 5 minutes or until cool. Beat in butter, a little at a time; stir in Amaretto. Chill until spreading consistency.

4. Assembly: Carefully remove meringue circles from parchment paper. Divide butter cream in half. Use half to ice two meringue circles; stack them on a serving platter. Top with last meringue circle; use remaining butter cream to ice top and sides. Crush meringue fingers; decorate top and sides with crushed meringue.

STRAWBERRY CREAM DACQUOISE (BOCCONE DOLCE)

SERVES 6 TO 8

Preheat oven to 275° F (140° C)

3 baking sheets lined with parchment paper

MERINGUE:

1 cup	egg whites (about 7 egg whites)	250 mL
1/4 tsp	cream of tartar	1 mL
2 cups	granulated sugar	500 mL

FILLING:

4 oz	semi-sweet chocolate, chopped	125 g
2 tbsp	water	25 mL
3 cups	whipping (35%) cream	750 mL
1/3 cup	sifted icing sugar	75 mL
2 1/4 cups	strawberries, sliced	550 mL

1. Using the base of an 8-inch (2 L) springform pan as a template, draw an 8-inch (20 cm) circle on each parchment-lined baking sheet. Butter and flour parchment paper.

2. Make the meringue: In a bowl, beat egg whites with cream of tartar until soft peaks form; gradually add sugar, beating until glossy, stiff peaks form. Spoon meringue onto circles on parchment paper, or pipe onto circles using a pastry bag. Bake 1 1/2 to 2 hours or until meringue is golden. Cool on wire racks.

3. Make the filling: In a bowl, melt the chocolate with water over hot (not boiling) water, stirring until smooth; set aside. In another bowl, whip cream until it starts to thicken; gradually add icing sugar, beating until stiff peaks form.

4. Assembly: Put one meringue circle on serving platter; spread with melted chocolate (reheat chocolate if too thick). Spread with whipped cream to 3/4-inch (2 cm) thickness; top with sliced strawberries. Repeat. Top with last meringue circle; ice top and sides with remaining whipped cream. Decorate with remaining strawberries and drizzle with remaining chocolate. Chill 2 hours before serving.

Sardi's — New York

CRÈME BRÛLÉE

SERVES 6

Preheat oven to 325° F (160° C)

Six 1/2 cup (125 mL) ramekins

1 1/2 cups	whipping (35%) cream	375 mL
1/2 cup	milk	125 mL
1/4 cup	granulated sugar	50 mL
1 tbsp	vanilla extract	15 mL
6	egg yolks	6
1/4 cup	granulated sugar	50 mL
2 tbsp	granulated sugar	25 mL

1. In a saucepan over medium heat, combine cream, milk, 1/4 cup (50 mL) sugar and vanilla; cook, stirring, until sugar dissolves. Remove from heat. In a bowl, whisk egg yolks with 1/4 cup (50 mL) sugar; gradually whisk in hot cream mixture. Pour mixture back into saucepan; cook over low heat a few minutes, stirring constantly, until slightly thickened. Pour into ramekins.

2. Set ramekins in a pan large enough to hold them; pour in enough hot water to come half way up sides. Bake 40 to 50 minutes or until set. Remove from water bath; cool on wire racks. Chill.

3. Set top oven rack as close to element as possible; preheat broiler. Sprinkle 1 tsp (5 mL) sugar over top of each custard. Cook until sugar melts and caramelizes. Serve immediately.

Gotham Bar & Grill - New York

Tulipe Cookie Cups filled with Ice Cream and Chocolate Sauce

Preheat oven to 375° F (190° C)

3 baking sheets, buttered and floured

Tulipe cookie cups:

1 cup	icing sugar	250 mL
1/3 cup	all-purpose flour	75 mL
1/4 cup	melted butter	50 mL
1/2 cup	egg whites (about 3 egg whites)	125 mL
3/4 tsp	vanilla extract	4 mL

Chocolate sauce:

3 oz	semi-sweet chocolate, chopped	90 g
3/4 cup	whipping (35%) cream	175 mL
6	large scoops ice cream	6
	Fresh berries (optional)	

1. Make the tulipe cookie cups: In a food processor, blend icing sugar with flour; beat in butter. Add egg whites and vanilla; blend until smooth. Drop batter onto prepared baking sheets in 2 tbsp (25 mL) amounts spaced well apart; with a knife spread batter thinly to a 6-inch (15 cm) circle. Repeat with remaining batter; you can fit two cookies on each sheet. Bake for 7 minutes or until golden. Quickly loosen each cookie and place each over bottom of a glass or bowl, squeezing to form tulip shape. Cool completely.

2. Make the chocolate sauce: In a bowl, melt chocolate over hot (not boiling) water, stirring until smooth; gradually stir in cream. Serve warm or cold.

3. Assembly: Put a large scoop of ice cream in each cookie cup. Drizzle with chocolate sauce. Decorate with berries, if desired.

La Tulipe – New York

MOCHA CRÈME BRÛLÉE

SERVES 6

Preheat oven to 325° F (160° C)
Six 1/2 cup (125 mL) ramekins

2 cups	whipping (35%) cream	500 mL
1 tbsp	instant espresso powder	15 mL
4	egg yolks	4
1/2 cup	granulated sugar	125 mL
1/4 cup	chocolate liqueur	50 mL
3/4 tsp	vanilla extract	4 mL
	Brown sugar	

1. In a saucepan, heat cream with espresso powder until almost boiling; remove from heat. In a bowl, beat egg yolks with sugar; gradually whisk in hot cream. Beat in chocolate liqueur and vanilla. Remove and discard any foam on top of custard. Pour into ramekins.

2. Set ramekins in pan large enough to hold them; pour in enough hot water to come half way up sides. Cover pan loosely with foil. Bake 45 to 60 minutes or until set. Remove from water bath; cool on wire racks. Chill.

3. Preheat oven to broil; set top rack as close to element as possible. Sprinkle some brown sugar over top of each custard. Cook until sugar melts and caramelizes. Serve immediately.

John Clancy's –
New York

CLASSIC BREAD PUDDING

SERVES 8

Preheat oven to 350° F (180° C)

8-inch (2 L) square baking pan, buttered and floured

BREAD PUDDING:

1 cup	raisins	250 mL
3	day-old rolls *or* 4 oz (125 g) day-old french bread, thinly sliced	3
2 cups	half-and-half (10%) cream	500 mL
4	egg yolks	4
1/3 cup	granulated sugar	75 mL
1 tsp	vanilla extract	5 mL
Half	apple, peeled, cored and thinly sliced	Half
1/2 cup	chopped nuts	125 mL
3 tbsp	butter	45 mL

VANILLA SAUCE:

1 cup	milk	250 mL
1 tbsp	vanilla extract	15 mL
3	egg yolks	3
1/3 cup	granulated sugar	75 mL
	Icing sugar	

1. Make bread pudding: Add warm water (or rum) to cover to raisins; set aside to soak. Lightly toast sliced bread; set aside. In a large bowl, whisk together cream, egg yolks, sugar and vanilla; stir in apples, nuts, drained raisins and toasted bread. Let stand 2 minutes. Stir and pour into prepared pan. Dot with butter.

2. Set pan in larger pan; pour in enough hot water to come 1-inch (2.5 cm) up sides. Bake 30 minutes. Remove pan from water bath; bake 15 minutes longer. Cool to room temperature on wire rack. Chill.

Chalet Suisse –
New York

3. Make the vanilla sauce: In a bowl, beat yolks with sugar until pale yellow and thick. In a saucepan, heat cream until almost boiling; remove from heat. Whisk a little of the hot cream into yolk mixture, then pour back into remaining cream. Whisk constantly over low heat until mixture is thick enough to coat a spoon; do not boil. Remove from heat; whisk in vanilla. Chill.

4. Serve bread pudding with vanilla sauce and dusted with sifted icing sugar.

DOUBLE CHOCOLATE CHUNK COOKIES

MAKES 24

TIP

Substitute 1 cup (250 mL) chocolate chips for the chocolate.

Try pecans instead of walnuts.

Preheat oven to 350° F (180° C)
2 baking sheets, buttered and floured

1 cup	butter, softened	250 mL
1 cup	granulated sugar	250 mL
1/2 cup	packed brown sugar	125 mL
1 tsp	vanilla extract	5 mL
1	egg	1
2 tbsp	milk	25 mL
1/3 cup	cocoa	75 mL
1 3/4 cups	all-purpose flour	425 mL
1/4 tsp	baking powder	1 mL
6 oz	semi-sweet chocolate, chopped	175 g
1 cup	chopped walnuts	250 mL

1. In a bowl, cream butter until very soft; beat in sugar, brown sugar and vanilla until fluffy. Beat in egg and milk; beat in cocoa until smooth. Stir in flour and baking powder just until blended. Fold in chocolate and walnuts.

2. Drop batter by rounded tablespoonsful onto baking sheets. Bake 11 to 13 minutes or until cake tester inserted in center comes out clean.

Peppermint Park –
New York

CREAM PUFFS WITH CANNOLI FILLING AND CHOCOLATE SAUCE

SERVES 8 TO 10

Preheat oven to 400° F (200° C)
Baking sheet, buttered and floured

CREAM PUFFS:

1/2 cup	water	125 mL
1/4 cup	butter	50 mL
1/2 tsp	salt	2 mL
1/2 cup	all-purpose flour	125 mL
3	eggs	3
	Granulated sugar	

FILLING:

2 cups	ricotta cheese	500 mL
2/3 cup	icing sugar	150 mL
1/2 cup	chocolate chips	125 mL
Pinch	cinnamon	Pinch
2 tbsp	minced candied fruit (optional)	25 mL

CHOCOLATE SAUCE:

3 oz	semi-sweet chocolate, chopped	90 g
3/4 cup	whipping (35%) cream	175 mL

1. Make the cream puffs: In a saucepan, bring water, butter and salt to a boil; remove from heat. Stir in flour all at once; cook over medium heat, stirring vigorously, 2 minutes or until pastry comes away from pan. Remove from heat. Beat in eggs, one at a time, beating well after each. Spoon mixture the size of walnuts onto baking sheet, or use piping bag. Sprinkle with sugar. Bake 20 to 25 minutes or until golden; do not open oven door while cream puffs bake. Cool on wire rack.

2. Make the filling: In a bowl, beat ricotta with icing sugar until smooth. Stir in chocolate chips, cinnamon and, if desired, candied fruit. Chill 10 minutes. Poke a small hole in the bottom of each cream puff; spoon in filling or pipe in using a pastry bag.

3. Make the chocolate sauce: In a bowl, melt chocolate over hot (not boiling) water, stirring until smooth; gradually stir in cream. Serve with filled cream puffs.

Ferrara – New York

SARABETH'S SCONES

MAKES ABOUT 10

Preheat oven to 350° F (180° C)
Baking sheet, buttered and floured

SCONES:

1 1/2 cups	all-purpose flour	375 mL
1 1/2 tsp	baking powder	7 mL
1 1/2 tsp	granulated sugar	7 mL
Pinch	salt	Pinch
1/4 cup	cold butter	50 mL
1/2 cup	currants	125 mL
1	egg	1
1/2 cup	milk	125 mL

EGG WASH:

1	egg	1
2 tbsp	milk	25 mL

1. Make the scones: In a bowl, stir together flour, baking powder, sugar and salt; with a pastry cutter or two knives, cut in butter until coarse crumb consistency. Stir in currants. In a separate bowl, whisk together egg and milk; stir into flour mixture just until mixed. On a floured surface pat dough out to 1-inch (2.5 cm) thickness. Using a 2-inch (5 cm) round cookie cutter, cut into scones; put on baking sheet. Reroll scraps and cut into scones.

2. Make the egg wash: In a small bowl whisk together egg and milk. Using a pastry brush, brush over scones. Bake 20 minutes or until golden.

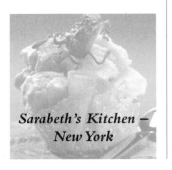

Sarabeth's Kitchen –
New York

TULIPE COOKIE CUPS FILLED WITH ICE CREAM AND CHOCOLATE SAUCE (PAGE 154) ➤

CHOCOLATE CHIP ALMOND COOKIES

MAKES ABOUT 30

Preheat oven to 350° F (180° C)

2 baking sheets, buttered

1 cup	butter, softened	250 mL
3/4 cup	packed brown sugar	175 mL
3/4 cup	granulated sugar	175 mL
2	eggs	2
1/2 tsp	vanilla extract	2 mL
1 3/4 cups	all–purpose flour	425 mL
1 tsp	baking soda	5 mL
3/4 tsp	salt	4 mL
2 cups	chocolate chips	500 mL
1 cup	toasted chopped almonds	250 mL

1. In a bowl, cream butter with brown sugar and sugar until fluffy; beat in eggs, one at a time, beating well after each. Beat in vanilla. In a separate bowl, stir together flour, baking soda and salt; stir into creamed mixture just until blended. Fold in chocolate chips and almonds.

2. Drop batter by rounded tablespoonsful onto prepared baking sheets. Bake 15 to 20 minutes or until golden. Cool on baking sheet on wire rack.

Sarabeth's Kitchen — New York

◄ RASPBERRY PYRAMID (PAGE 168)

SOUR CREAM AND CHOCOLATE BROWNIES

SERVES 16

Preheat oven to 325° F (160° C)

8-inch (2 L) square pan, buttered and floured

8 oz	semi-sweet chocolate, chopped	250 g
2	eggs	2
3/4 cup	granulated sugar	175 mL
1/2 cup	melted butter	125 mL
1/3 cup	sour cream	75 mL
2 tsp	vanilla extract	10 mL
3/4 cup	all-purpose flour	175 mL
1 tsp	baking powder	5 mL
1/2 cup	chocolate chips (optional)	125 mL

1. In a bowl, melt the chocolate over hot (not boiling) water, stirring until smooth; cool slightly, then beat in eggs. In a separate bowl, stir together sugar and melted butter; beat into chocolate mixture. Beat in sour cream and vanilla.

2. In another bowl, stir together flour and baking powder; stir into chocolate mixture just until mixed. If desired, fold in chocolate chips. Pour into prepared pan. Bake 25 to 30 minutes or until slightly soft just at center. Cool in pan on wire rack.

Carole's Cheesecake Co. - Toronto

ESPRESSO AND SAMBUCCA BRÛLÉE

SERVES 6

Preheat oven to 350° F (180° C)

Six 1/2-cup (125 mL) ramekins

1 1/2 cups	whipping (35%) cream	375 mL
1/2 cup	espresso or strong coffee	125 mL
1/4 cup	Sambucca *or* other licorice liqueur	50 mL
3 tbsp	granulated sugar	45 mL
4	egg yolks	4
2	eggs	2
	brown sugar	

1. In a bowl, whisk together cream, coffee, Sambuca, sugar, egg yolks and eggs. Pour into ramekins. Set ramekins in pan large enough to hold them; pour in enough hot water to come half way up sides. Cover pan loosely with foil. Bake 20 to 30 minutes or until center is set. Remove from water bath; cool on wire rack. Chill.

2. Set top oven rack as close to element as possible; pre-heat broiler. Sprinkle some brown sugar over top of each custard. Cook until sugar melts and caramelizes. Serve immediately.

Fenton's – Toronto

GÂTEAU ST-HONORÉ

SERVES 8 TO 10

TIP

Instead of, or in addition to, the caramelized sugar, you can serve this with chocolate sauce, either prepared or homemade (see recipe for TULIPE COOKIE CUPS FILLED WITH ICE CREAM AND CHOCOLATE SAUCE, page 154).

Preheat oven to 400° F (200° C)
Large baking sheet, buttered and floured

PASTRY:

1/2 cup	water	125 mL
1/4 cup	butter	50 mL
1/2 tsp	salt	2 mL
1/3 cup	all-purpose flour	75 mL
3	eggs	3
	Granulated sugar	

PASTRY CREAM FILLING:

1	egg	1
1/4 cup	granulated sugar	50 mL
2 tbsp	all-purpose flour	25 mL
1 cup	milk	250 mL
1/2 tsp	vanilla extract	2 mL
1 cup	whipping (35%) cream	250 mL
1 1/2 tbsp	kirsch	22 mL

CARAMELIZED SUGAR (OPTIONAL):

1/2 cup	granulated sugar	125 mL
2 tbsp	water	25 mL
3	drops lemon juice	3

1. Make the pastry: In a saucepan, bring water, butter and salt to a boil; remove from heat. Stir in flour all at once; cook over medium heat, stirring vigorously, 2 minutes or until pastry comes away from pan. Remove from heat. Beat in eggs, one at a time, beating well after each. Spoon mixture the size of walnuts onto baking sheet, or use piping bag. Sprinkle with sugar. Bake 20 to 25 minutes or until golden; do not open oven door while they bake. Cool on wire rack.

Patachou – Toronto

2. Make the pastry cream: In a bowl, beat egg. In another bowl, stir together sugar and flour. In a saucepan, heat milk and vanilla until almost boiling; whisk into flour mixture, then pour back into saucepan. Cook over medium heat, stirring constantly, until mixture boils. Whisk a little of the hot milk mixture into egg; pour back into saucepan, whisking constantly, over medium–low heat until mixture thickens (do not boil). Pour into a bowl; lay piece of plastic wrap on surface of pastry cream. Chill.

3. In a bowl, whip cream until stiff; stir in kirsch. Fold one-third of whipped cream into chilled pastry cream; set aside remaining whipped cream. Poke a small hole in the bottom of each cream puff; spoon in pastry cream filling or pipe in using a pastry bag. Arrange on serving platter in circular fashion. Spoon remaining whipped cream into center or pipe in using a pastry bag.

4. Make caramelized sugar, if desired: In a saucepan, cook sugar and water over medium heat, stirring to dissolve. Add lemon juice; bring to a boil. Cook until mixture turns light brown, about 5 minutes; do not let sugar turn dark brown. Pour into a bowl; spoon over puffs. Serve dessert the same day.

CRÈME CARAMEL

SERVES 6

Preheat oven to 325° F (160° C)
Six 1/2-cup (125 mL) ramekins

1/2 cup	granulated sugar	125 mL
3	drops lemon juice	3
3	eggs	3
2	egg yolks	2
1/2 cup	granulated sugar	125 mL
1 tbsp	grated orange rind	15 mL
1/2 tsp	vanilla extract	2 mL
2 cups	milk	500 mL
	Fresh berries (optional)	
	Whipped cream (optional)	

1. In a saucepan, combine 1/2 cup (125 mL) sugar and lemon juice; bring to a boil. Boil until light brown; do not let sugar turn dark brown. Quickly divide among ramekins, tilting each to coat bottom and sides.

2. In a bowl, whisk together eggs, egg yolks, sugar, orange rind and vanilla. In a saucepan, heat milk until almost boiling; whisk into egg mixture. Pour into ramekins.

3. Set ramekins in pan large enough to hold them; pour in enough hot water to come half way up sides. Bake 40 to 50 minutes or until set. Remove from water bath; cool on wire rack. Chill.

4. To serve, run knife around inside edges of ramekins; invert onto individual dessert plates. If desired, decorate with berries or whipped cream.

Paul's French Foods –
Toronto

SNOW EGGS
(OEUFS À LA NEIGE)

SERVES 4

TIP

If you prefer, you can poach the snow eggs in simmering water rather than milk.

CRÈME ANGLAISE:

4	egg yolks	4
1/2 cup	granulated sugar	125 mL
2 cups	half-and-half (10%) cream *or* table (18%) cream	500 mL
1 tsp	vanilla extract	5 mL

SNOW EGGS:

2 cups	milk	500 mL
3	egg whites	3
6 tbsp	granulated sugar	90 mL
	chopped pistachio nuts (optional)	

1. Make the *crème anglaise*: In a bowl, beat yolks with sugar until pale yellow and thick. In a saucepan, heat cream until almost boiling; remove from heat. Whisk a little of hot cream into yolk mixture, then pour back into saucepan. Whisk constantly over low heat until mixture is thick enough to coat a spoon; do not boil. Remove from heat; whisk in vanilla. Chill.

2. Make the snow eggs: In a large saucepan, heat milk over medium heat. In a bowl, beat egg whites until soft peaks form; gradually add sugar, beating until stiff peaks form. With a large serving spoon, form 4 egg-shaped meringues; gently drop into simmering milk. Poach 2 minutes; turn over and poach another minute or until firm. Remove with a slotted spoon; drain on paper towels.

3. Divide cold *crème anglaise* among 4 individual dessert bowls. Top with a snow egg. Chill until ready to serve. If desired, serve sprinkled with chopped pistachio nuts.

Fenton's — Toronto

RASPBERRY PYRAMID

SERVES 6

TIP

The wafer batter will keep, covered and stored in the refrigerator, a few days — bake only as many as you need (four per serving).

Preheat oven to 425° F (220° C)
Two large baking sheets, buttered and floured

PISTACHIO NUT WAFERS:

1 cup	all-purpose flour	250 mL
1/2 cup	icing sugar	125 mL
4	egg whites, beaten	4
2 tbsp	honey	25 mL
2 1/2 tbsp	butter	37 mL
	Pistachio nuts, finely chopped	

CRÈME ANGLAISE:

3	egg yolks	3
2 tbsp	granulated sugar	25 mL
1 cup	milk	250 mL
1/2 tsp	vanilla extract	2 mL
1 cup	whipping (35%) cream	250 mL
1 tbsp	icing sugar	15 mL
2 1/4 cups	raspberries	550 mL
	Icing sugar	
	Chopped pistachio nuts	

1. Make the wafers: In a bowl, blend flour, icing sugar, egg whites and honey; melt butter and stir in while still hot. Stir in pistachio nuts. Drop batter onto prepared baking sheets in 2 tsp (10 mL) amounts spaced well apart; with a knife spread batter thinly to circles 3 inches (7.5 cm) in diameter. Bake for 5 minutes or until golden. Remove from pan; cool on wire rack. Butter and flour baking sheets again and repeat with remaining batter.

2. Make the *crème anglaise*: In a bowl, beat yolks with sugar until pale yellow and thick. In a saucepan, heat milk until almost boiling; remove from heat. Whisk a little of the hot milk into yolk mixture, then pour back into saucepan. Whisk constantly over low heat until mixture is thick enough to coat a spoon; do not boil. Remove from heat; whisk in vanilla. Chill.

Sutton Place – Toronto

3. In a bowl, whip cream until it starts to thicken; gradually add icing sugar, beating until stiff peaks form. Set aside.

4. Assembly: Spoon a bit of *crème anglaise* onto each individual dessert plate. Put a wafer on top, spread with whipped cream and top with a few raspberries. Repeat twice. Top with a wafer, dust with sifted icing sugar and sprinkle with chopped pistachio nuts.

KAHLUA CREAM DREAM

Preheat oven to 350° F (180° C)

2 baking sheets lined with buttered, floured parchment paper

CHOCOLATE LAYERS:

2	eggs	2
4	egg yolks	4
1/2 cup	granulated sugar	125 mL
3 tbsp	all-purpose flour	45 mL
1 tbsp	cocoa	15 mL

MERINGUE:

6	egg whites	6
1/2 cup	granulated sugar	125 mL

FILLING:

2 cups	whipping (35%) cream	500 mL
1	pkg (1 tbsp [7 g]) gelatin	1
1/2 cup	Kahlua *or* other coffee flavored liqueur	125 mL
	Icing sugar	
	Chocolate shavings (optional)	

1. Make the chocolate layers: In a bowl, beat eggs, egg yolks and sugar until pale yellow and thickened. Sift in flour and cocoa; stir to blend. Set aside.

2. Make the meringue: In a bowl, beat egg whites until soft peaks form; gradually add sugar, beating until stiff peaks form. Fill pastry bag with mixture. Pipe 5 rows of meringue down the length of each baking sheet, 1 inch (2.5 cm) wide and spaced 1-inch (2.5 cm) apart. Rinse out pastry bag; fill with cocoa batter. Pipe five rows of cocoa batter down the length of each baking sheet, filling in spaces between meringue rows. Bake 10 to 15 minutes or until golden. Cool on baking sheets on wire rack.

Mövenpick – Toronto

3. Make the filling: In a bowl, whip cream until stiff peaks form. Dissolve gelatin in water according to package directions; cool slightly. Fold gelatin and Kahlua into whipped cream.

4. Assembly: Dust two clean tea towels with sifted icing sugar. Invert baking sheets onto tea towels; remove baking sheet and carefully peel off parchment paper. Cut each layer in half crosswise. On a serving platter layer the 4 pieces, spreading each layer with filling and icing the entire layer cake with remaining filling. If desired, decorate with chocolate shavings.

RESTAURANT/CHEF PROFILES

The desserts presented in this book were originally selected from the offerings of top establishments in the US and Canada, adapted for home cooking, and published in two books in 1988 and 1989. The following profiles have been excerpted from those original publications. Since it is a fact of today's hospitality business that establishments come and go, you may find references here to restaurants and/or pastry chefs whose circumstances have changed. The recipes they inspired, however, like all those in this book, continue to stand as classics.

A PIECE OF CAKE, TORONTO

Formerly located in the heart of Toronto's fashionable Bay/Bloor area, this café was a favorite of the after-theater and movie crowd. Originally from Hungary, Pastry Chef Andre Szilagy created about 40 different desserts, varying weekly.

AURORA, NEW YORK

Celestial inspiration may have been responsible for this classy French bar-restaurant, named after the deity, and producing such heavenly delights as apple tart and a delicate apricot mousse with substance.

BAKER STREET, TORONTO

The creation of Esther Kravice and Mary Somerton, two sisters crazy about desserts, Baker Street began as a home-based business catering to the enormous demand for good pastries. The response to their extraordinary desserts has been tremendous — look for their Kahlua Truffle Cake and Raspberry Bombe.

BETWEEN THE BREAD, NEW YORK

Dishes that appeal to the eye, tantalize the taste buds, incite the olfactory nerve to waves of pleasure. All this and sane prices too. A selection of homey and old-fashioned desserts includes a crunchy yet melt-in-your-mouth Walnut Lemon Butter Tart.

CARNEGIE DELICATESSEN, New York

For anyone unfamiliar with this continuously popular New York institution, the Carnegie Deli was the set for Woody Allen's film, *Broadway Danny Rose*. Here regulars enjoy outrageous helpings of Carnegie's Famous Cheesecake.

CAROLE'S CHEESECAKE CO., Toronto

No name in Toronto is more synonymous with exciting high-quality cheesecakes than Carole Ogus. Taught to cook by her husband, she began experimenting with baking, creating such fabulous desserts that friends started asking her to bake for social functions. Carole now has franchises throughout Ontario.

CHALET SUISSE, New York

Under executive chef, Dietmar Schlueter, here's an eatery that has turned out consistently wonderful meals and scrumptious desserts. Chocolate is a Swiss institution and the dessert menu reflects that. The Chocolate Fondue is creamy and sharply-sweet.

THE COURTYARD CAFÉ, Toronto

Pastry chef Norbert Maushagen kept his desserts looking and tasting among the best in the city. His specialties given to the book include some of the best parfaits ever created. Bon appetit!

DESSERT PEDDLER, Unionville

Mary Ann Moran, like many other successful women in the food trade, began working out of her home. She eventually was forced to open a storefront herself, offering good old-fashioned desserts like butter tarts, Nanaimo bars, carrot cake, and chocolate cake.

DUFFLET PASTRIES, Toronto

Dufflet Rosenberg is synonymous with decadent and beautiful desserts. She opened her famous retail spot on Queen Street in 1980 and in 1985 set up facilities in a factory for the wholesale trade, the mainstay of her business.

FENTON'S, Toronto

Werner Bassen, Fenton's original pastry chef, began his career at the age of 14 as a cook in Germany. He entered into the pastry end of the business; His White and Dark Chocolate Pâté, among other recipes here, is incredibly simple and elegant.

FERRARA, NEW YORK

Of the many old-world style desserts available, Ferrara offers some of its most popular. Everybody loves cream puffs. Try Cream Puffs with Cannoli filling; the flavor is unusual. Almond Ricotta Cheesecake is a light cheesecake with an exceptionally creamy texture and delicate almond taste. Delizioso!

THE FOUR SEASONS, NEW YORK

The eclectic menu changes (as you might expect) seasonally. Dishes delight the eye and dazzle the palate. Desserts like Chocolate Velvet Cake are dense, moist and lush.

THE FOUR SEASONS YORKVILLE, TORONTO

This elegant hotel's dining-room, Truffles, features Austrian chef Wolfgang von Wieser. Wolfgang apprenticed in Switzerland and then worked at numerous five-star hotels. Try his Raspberry Mousse on an Orange Cream Cheese Gratin.

FRASER MORRIS FINE FOODS, NEW YORK

Long before gourmet-to-go was the norm, Fraser Morris Fine Foods had been on the indefatigable search for unique ways to tantalize the palate. For half a century the discriminating tastes of New York's first families have been catered to here.

GINDI, NEW YORK

Francine Gindi's career as a pastry chef has led her to some of the best restaurants in the city. When she opened Gindi in 1982, her desserts were already so popular that the shop was greeted with rave reviews from every food critic in town. Try the Chocolate Pecan Pie

GOTHAM, NEW YORK

Classic desserts live side by side with zesty new creations at the Gotham Bar & Grill. Try the creamy Crème Brûlée or the refreshing Five Fruit and Berry Compote. Both are easy to create, a light and lively ending for any meal.

LES DÈLICES GUY PASCAL, NEW YORK

Throughout the day and evening an artful display of rich pastries fills immaculate glass cases. Gorgeous cakes, glistening fruit tarts, chocolate mousse and delightful little cookies-everything is sinfully delicious and tempting. Try the layered Mousse Cake combining perennial favorites — orange and chocolate.

INN ON THE PARK, TORONTO

Pastry chef Sitram Sharma left Guyana in 1970 in order to study English. His love and expertise lie in sugar and chocolate work and he has won gold medals at food and wine shows for his spectacular creations.

JOHN CLANCY'S, NEW YORK

Desserts here have a distinctly American feel. Any one of these will appeal: Chocolate Cream Roulade, a round of sponge cake and chocolate coffee; Bourbon Pecan Tart, a taste of the old south at its finest; Mocha Crème Brûlée for an unusual custard; or the luscious Almond Pear Cream Tart.

JUST DESSERTS, TORONTO

Rick Sanders took a substantial risk some 20 years ago when he opened Toronto's first dessert café. But today Just Desserts has some 10 locations in Toronto alone. Try one of the best old fashioned chocolate cakes ever created.

KING EDWARD HOTEL, TORONTO

With French chef, Joel Gaillot, in charge of desserts, the King Edward Hotel's famous Café Victoria has attracted plenty of attention from devotees who clamor for his creative desserts.

W.D. KONES, TORONTO

John Matheson and Bob Duncan had always been ice cream addicts. So it wasn't surprising that their company, W.D. Kones, offered a repertoire of some 40 different flavors.

LAFAYETTE (THE DRAKE HOTEL), NEW YORK

Master chef Louis Outhier is consulting chef at Lafayette. In Europe, Outhier is famous for L'Oasis, La Napoule, on the Riviera, long one of France's elite restaurants. At Lafayette he has created a superb table d'hôte with a nod towards Southeast Asian spicing. Try the Mango Strudel with Kiwi Sauce.

L'HÔTEL, TORONTO

L'Hôtel features the exquisite Chantarelle dining room and one of Toronto's most beautiful garden coffee shops, the Orchard Café, where Philippe Egalon's creations can be seen and eaten daily. He has won numerous awards for his sugar work, including a gold and silver medal at the Food and Wine Show.

LA RÉSERVE, New York

La Réserve is the marvelous creation of Jean-Louis Missud. This French salute to gastronomie is a haven for culinary purists. Pick out the subtle flavors in the Hazelnut Buttercream Cake with Anise. The Tarte Tartin will please the most discriminating guests.

LA TULIPE, New York

La Tulipe is a cosy restaurant/bistro housed in a brownstone. One rich dessert is Tulipe Cookie cups filled with ice cream and chocolate sauce. The light and tempting Lemon Chiffon Tart cools any palate. A sure pleaser.

LE BERNARDIN, New York

The French love to take the ordinary and transform it into the extraordinary. At Le Bernardin appearance and arrangement of desserts equal the importance of taste. Here's a Fruit Soup that can start or finish a meal. Made with fresh fruit and orange cream, it is a spectacular creation no one will be able to resist.

LE CIRQUE, New York

Desserts are legendary at Le Cirque, which provides one of the finest selections in the city. Crème Brûlée — custard sprinkled with sugar and passed beneath a broiler until browned — is the specialty and utterly delicious. Try the Crisp Millefeuille with Fresh Fruit from the restaurant with a reputation for its continual ability to captivate patrons.

LE CYGNE, New York

Dining at the classic French restaurant, Le Cygne, recalls more than the grace and beauty of the swan, the bird for which it is named. For the ultimate in richness and freshness, the lighter-than-air Raspberry Mousse can't be equalled.

LUTÈCE, New York

André Soltner, chef-proprietaire, is nearly single-handedly responsible for an atmosphere of refinement in which exceptional dishes are offered with reverence. Haute cuisine is at home here, as are proud but simple desserts. Hot Apple Charlotte is are rich fruity delight for all occasions, as is the Apple Cream Pie. As a special treat for family and friends, serve them the Orange Cream Tart. Bon appetit!

MISS GRIMBLE, New York

A staggering display of mouth-watering sweets tempts and tantalizes. The Apple Raisin Tart tastes like the kind Grandma baked. And for bakers who have always longed to try a cheesecake recipe but never quite found the courage, Miss Grimble's ABC Cheesecake is a cinch.

MÖVENPICK, Toronto

Executive pastry chef Shelley Beeston, a native Torontonian, studied graphic arts at a local community college. But her love for baking and pastries led her away to the practical world of desserts. Tasting one of her creations is quite an experience.

NANCY'S CHOCOLATES, Toronto

Nancy Gangbar's love of chocolate and artistry encouraged her to open Bear Essentials, located in the Forest Hill area of Toronto. Her products range through every type of truffle imaginable, from cookies and chocolates to personalized chocolate baskets.

PATACHOU, Toronto

Featuring exquisite French pastry, Patachou has two successful locations in Toronto. Chef Christian Serebecbere provides us with some very special desserts from among the best of his classical French creations. Try his easy Gâteau St. Honoré.

PAUL'S FRENCH FOODS, Toronto

Pastry chef Max Wirth, was born in Switzerland. He did his training near Zurich and worked for many exclusive European hotels and bakeries before coming to Toronto. His truffle cake and mousse cake have always been favorites.

PEPPERMINT PARK, New York

Kamel Mahmoud, premier ice cream maker and cake decorator, churns out over 100 buckets of New York's finest ice cream each day. In addition, sherbets and sorbets are served, enormous banana splits, thick milk shakes, and 10 fruity flavors of yogurt.

THE PLAZA, New York

Pastry chef Eric Bedoucha, in charge of all desserts at The Plaza, recommends the light and airy Raspberry Truffle Cake or, for a change of pace, the Apricot Walnut Cake, with its solid nutty goodness.

THE QUILTED GIRAFFE, NEW YORK

Desserts here are the pinnacle of a spontaneous menu. You can try the Grand Dessert, a sampling of every sweet available on any particular evening. But you'll probably want to stick with just one — like the White and Dark Chocolate Marbled Mousse Cake.

THE RAINBOW ROOM, NEW YORK

The Rainbow Room is perhaps the last of the formal supper clubs. Desserts, too, have an aura of splendor about them. Sample the Baked Alaska with Fruit Sauce — it will linger in your memory long after it's gone.

SARABETH'S KITCHEN, NEW YORK

Sarabeth's Kitchen is like grandma's country kitchen. The scent of baked goods wafts through the air. Jars and bottles of homemade jams and jellies entice. For breakfast, try Sarabeth's recipe for Scones.

SARDI'S, NEW YORK

Food in this theatrical ambiance leans towards the dramatic. Continental cuisine is served with a flair by clippy, city-smart waiters. When it comes to desserts, the Strawberry Cream Dacquoise is a long-running hit. For simpler tastes, try Date Rice Pudding.

THE SILVER PALATE, NEW YORK

It's may be that the tiniest gourmet food shop in the world is tucked away in Manhattan. Look for super desserts here, like the perpetually popular Chocolate Mousse Cake. And it is exceptional. Another chocolate delight is the Chocolate Chip Crumb Cake — easy to make and quick to disappear.

SUTTON PLACE, TORONTO

Brian Morin is one of the few native Torontonians working as a top pastry chefs in that city. His specialty and first love is plaited desserts, of which he is justifiably proud. He also loves preparing soufflés — as his classic Grand Marnier Soufflé attests.

SWEET SUE PASTRIES, NEW YORK

Sue Devor has always loved working with food, even when she was raising her five children. She began baking in her home for restaurants and became so successful that she opened her own shop to meet customer demand.

TAVERN ON THE GREEN, NEW YORK

Cuisine ranges from trendy to traditional, hot to cold dishes. A selection of fantastic desserts includes Chocolate Macadamia Nut Cake, a tribute to Hawaii's best; an Iced Lemon Soufflé that will thrill guests; and the elegant White Chocolate Mousse Layer Cake with Raspberries, an exquisite dream.

WINDOWS ON THE WORLD, NEW YORK

Out-of-this-galaxy delectables abound at this lofty (107 floors up, atop the World Trade Center), particularly the dreamy Amaretto Cheesecake.

INDEX

D

E